INTRODUS0-ARO-321

By T.J. Rohleder

Thank you for investing in this book. As you'll see, you are in for quite a surprise!

In a minute, I'll tell you more about what you're about to discover by carefully going through this book.

But for now, let me start off by asking you this question:

Did you know there are only 3 ways to make money?

YES, only 3.

Here they are:

METHOD #1:

You can sell your time for money.

This is the way 99% of the people make almost all of their money. Everyone from day laborers, who slave under the hot sun for minimum wage, to brain surgeons who get paid thousands of dollars an hour. All of these people are selling their time for money.

METHOD #2:

You can sell a product or service or a combination of both.

With this second method, your money comes from the sale of some product or service, <u>not</u> the amount of time you work. **This is a much smarter way to make money!** In fact, the world is filled with many millionaires who make almost all of their money with this second powerful method!

But the real secret to getting rich is to use the final method.

Just look...

METHOD #3:

PASSIVE INCOME! You use your money to make you even more money!

The 2nd method is quite capable of making you very rich. **But the third method of making money has made more people wealthy than the other two combined!** With this final method, you are putting your money into income-producing assets that automatically make you more money... All you do is sit back and cash the checks you receive from all of your investments!

And now for the best news:

Our $100,000 A MONTH SYSTEM is one of the most powerful ways to make money in the entire world because <u>ALL</u> of the money you can make will come from the 2nd and 3rd methods which are responsible for the GIANT fortunes that are made by the world's richest people!

(A) All of your wealth is generated from the sale of the high-dollar products and services that have a high perceived value and can pay you huge profits!

But you will <u>not</u> be selling these high-profit products and services yourself!

(B) **All of the sales are made for you by our powerful sales material and our expertly trained staff!**

(C) Plus, on top of all of this, you also have the rare ability to get paid a potential fortune from the time, work, and money of as many as hundreds or even thousands of other people!

When you fully understand how all of this is designed to make you a fortune – and add it all together – you'll see why I call our

"One of the world's greatest ways to become a millionaire!"

This gives you the ultimate way to cash-in with the same two methods that all of the world's richest people use to make their fortunes! **The amount of money you can earn has nothing to do with the amount of actual time and work you put in.**

And this leads to the biggest benefit of all...

Because we can run all of this for you — it is possible for you to make tens of thousands of dollars a month <u>without</u> doing any work!

Yes, I know how absolutely unbelievable that sounds — and BOLD statements such as this should make you very skeptical... After all, sitting back and getting paid tens of thousands of dollars a month does sound way too good to be true!

But this is exactly what our $100,000 A MONTH SYSTEM is designed to do for you!

Of course, there are <u>no</u> promises nor guarantees that you <u>will</u> make one hundred thousand dollars a month or any specific sum of money for doing absolutely no work — but the potential to get paid many thousands of dollars for letting us run everything for you is definitely here!

Here's why:

1. Your income comes from the sale of the high-dollar, high-profit products and services.

2. The sales material, our proven methods, and our expertly trained staff do all of the selling for you!

3. And you also have the amazing opportunity to get paid from as many as hundreds or even thousands of other people who can also be using the same exact 100%

duplicatable system that <u>you</u> are using to make all of your money!

Okay – that brings me to an important point...

Our $100,000 A MONTH SYSTEM is <u>not</u> multi-level marketing.

This has nothing to do with the methods that traditional multi-level or network marketing companies use. If you knew me, you would know that **I have a deep-seated hatred and terrible resentment against most traditional network or multi-level marketing companies.** There are so many problems associated with these companies – I could write a book about it! Oh wait! I <u>did</u> write a book about it! I wrote it in the early 2000's. It's called:

<u>MLM Sucks!</u>

I am in the process of re-writing this classic bestseller right now. It is filled with all kinds of reasons why traditional multi-level marketing is a complete rip-off for most people.

But there are a few things I <u>do</u> love about MLM...

- I love the idea of "people helping other people."

- I love any wealth-making method that lets the average person make money from the efforts of other people.

As for everything else about MLM or network marketing – I hate it all:

- I hate the complicated marketing plans that are designed to only make money for the companies themselves or the heavy hitters.

- I hate all of the personal selling that must be done.

- I hate all of the lies and deception that runs rampant in most MLM organizations.

Now here is the most exciting thing...

Our $100,000 A MONTH SYSTEM gives you all of the greatest benefits of Direct Response Marketing and Network Marketing – without any of the side effects!

This is designed to let you sit back and make a fortune from the time, work, money, and expert skills of as many as hundreds, or perhaps even thousands, of other people!

The more you understand this – the more _thrilled_ you will be!

So please read this book carefully. If you are as serious as I believe you are about making money, you will be _SHOCKED_ and _AMAZED_ before you are halfway through!

But for right now, let me tell you a little about me...

OUR RAGS-TO-RICHES STORY

For many years my wife, Eileen, and I struggled for every dollar. We never had enough money to pay all of our bills. Our life was a constant frustration. We were poverty poor. And we had no hope of getting out of our poverty.

- We had _no_ special education.

- We were _not_ born into a family that had a lot of money.

- We had _no_ special skills or knowledge.

- We had _none_ of the things that you need to get rich!

But we did have _one_ thing going for us...

We _hated_ our lives of poverty and we were convinced that there was something better out there for us. We were proud to be Americans and we firmly believed in this great country and _all_ of the opportunities that were available to average people like us.

Eileen and I _knew_ that other average people who had _less_ going for them than we had were getting rich! We heard all of the rags-to-riches stories of people who had started with very little or even no money and turned it into a huge fortune. And somewhere along the line we started to believe that it was more than possible to make a lot of money. <u>So</u> <u>we</u> <u>took</u> <u>BOLD</u> <u>action</u> <u>on</u> <u>our</u> <u>dreams</u> <u>of</u> <u>getting</u> <u>rich</u>!

<u>Here's</u> <u>what</u> <u>we</u> <u>did</u>... > We started to send away for <u>every</u> moneymaking program we could find that sounded different and was inexpensive. > We joined a bunch of multi-level marketing companies. > We began listening to motivational cassette tapes and reading all of the success books that we could get our hands on.

All of this fanned the flames of our desire!

It was like throwing a 55-gallon drum of jet fuel onto a raging fire! Now our belief that we could actually get rich turned into an obsession!

I call it "my magnificent obsession!" **And to make a long story short — within <u>less</u> than a handful of years — we became millionaires!**

Yes, all of our biggest dreams of making a fortune came true! In fact, when the riches began coming to us, they came so fast that we thought we were dreaming! *On more than one occasion we would look at each other and just start laughing uncontrollably!* We would literally pinch ourselves to make sure this was really happening.

And it <u>was</u> happening!

In fact, within 4 years from the time things started turning around for us, we made almost $10,000,000.00!

But wait a minute. **Please do <u>not</u> think for a single second that I'm bragging — because I'm <u>not</u>!**

We all know people who try to show off all of the time — and I can't stand being around these people. I'm sure <u>you</u> feel the same way.

No, I'm not bragging about the millions of dollars that came pouring into our lives within a few short years. <u>NO</u> <u>WAY</u>! **In fact, the only reason I am telling you our rags-to-riches story is to help you realize that the same thing can happen to you!**

Yes, it is possible for <u>you</u> to get very rich in a short period of time – just like we did!

In fact, I will be as bold as saying this...

I firmly believe that <u>you</u> could end up making even more money than we made!

All you have to do is discover the perfect opportunity that is designed to make you a fast fortune! Just find the right opportunity at the <u>right</u> time and get the right help from the right people – and <u>you</u> will have the amazing power to make millions... just like we did!

I firmly believe that our revolutionary new $100,000.00 A MONTH SYSTEM can be the perfect opportunity that turns everything around for you – just like our first discovery made us instant millionaires! I also believe that many of the people who get involved with us will make many tens of thousands of dollars a month with the secrets in this $100,000.00 A MONTH SYSTEM... and YOU can be one of these lucky people!

So please read this book carefully and prove to yourself that this really is the ultimate way to get rich from the comfort and privacy of your own home. Then discover how our ONE STEP MARKETING SYSTEM is designed to pay you huge sums of money for simply mailing some postcards, running a few small ads, or letting our expert suppliers do all of this for you!

So with all of this in mind, please...

Get Started Right Away!

You have proven how serious you are about making money by investing in this *How To Make $900.00 A Day Without Doing <u>Any</u> Work!* book... Now take the next step. Start by reading this entire book. This shows you the main reasons why this is the ultimate money-making discovery that we have made since we first began researching business opportunities back in 1988... I hope you will read all 99 of the powerful MILLIONAIRE SECRETS in this book by starting with #1 and then keep reading until you get to the end. Do this, and by the time you're finished with this book, you'll be so excited that you may need a pill to get to sleep tonight!

As you will soon see, our $100,000.00 A MONTH SYSTEM is the ultimate win/win partnership between you and me. The more I can do to help you make money, the more money I can make. This gives me the greatest incentive and reward to do everything possible to help you make the largest sum of money, in the fastest period of time, with the least amount of effort!

So THANK YOU once again for investing in this new book. I know you're going to be extremely excited when you begin to understand how simple and easy it is to get paid huge sums of automatic money! Please go over everything carefully. Then let us hear from you right away. I hope to meet you in person in the near future and have you tell me how this new discovery was the one Program that turned everything around for you!

99 Secrets To Help You Become A Millionaire In No Time Flat!

■ MILLIONAIRE SECRET #1

How To Make Thousands Of Dollars Very Quickly!

The secret to making thousands of dollars in the quickest period of time is simple: 1. Just find a proven secret that is making other people thousands of dollars. **2.** Then discover EXACTLY what they are doing to make all of their money. **3.** Then find as many ways as you can to duplicate their success and correct any mistakes that they're making. That's it. This is all you do to put huge sums of money in your pocket in the fastest period of time! Sounds simple, doesn't it? Well it is simple! But don't let the simplicity fool you. You see, if one average person can make huge sums of money with some type of business, then you can, too! Remember that. Ideas are transferable. All you have to do to get rich is duplicate the methods that other people are using to get rich... Just do more of whatever they're doing and correct the mistakes they're making. This simple formula lets you make as much or even more money than they're making.

This is the secret we use to discover the hottest secrets that make other people very rich!

Our company has been researching business and money-making opportunities since 1988... We look for the best ideas that other people are using to make huge sums of money... We gather all of the facts... We discover what they're doing right and what they're doing wrong. Then we simply duplicate the things that they're doing right and correct all of the mistakes that they're making... It's so simple and easy and yet it can make you a fortune!

This is how we discovered our '$100,000 A MONTH SYSTEM!' Our research led us to a group of average people who were already making over $50,000.00 to $100,000.00 a month... We discovered how these people are getting paid huge sums of daily cash – while automatically building up a steady stream of monthly income that keeps growing bigger! We also discovered that many of the people who were <u>brand new</u> to this opportunity were already getting paid thousands of dollars! Plus, I was <u>SHOCKED</u> to find that many of the people who were making thousands of dollars a month had <u>no</u> previous business experience! Then we discovered what they were doing right and wrong. Then we simply eliminated the things they were doing wrong and presto! Now we had a simple and easy system to instantly make many thousands of dollars for all of the people who wanted to make super fast cash! Easy, isn't it?

■ MILLIONAIRE SECRET #2

This Amazing Wealth Secret That Can Make You Thousands Of Dollars A Month <u>Without</u> Talking To Anyone!

You've heard the quote: "Nobody makes any money until it's sold." It's true! Selling is the key to making money... It's the salespeople in every company who make the cash register sing! These people make all of the other jobs possible. In fact, everyone owe their jobs to the people who do all of the selling.

But personal selling sucks! I can't think of a worse way to make money than trying to convince people to buy your products and services... This is a very hard way to make money. I know. For years I was a salesman and faced rejection every single day. I had doors slammed in my face and was hung up on every single day of the week. It was a terrible way to make a living and I hated it! You probably do, too. Have you ever tried to make money by selling? If so, you know that this is a very hard way of life. You have to deal with all kinds of negativity from people who do not want to give you the time of day. No matter how much your product or service can help them, they don't care. They don't want to listen to anything you have to say. They are rude to you and treat you with zero respect. It's hard to pump yourself up every day of the week while you are getting beat down. Most people burn out after a few months or years. They simply can't handle it.

But there is a way to sell without talking to a single soul, it's called Direct Response Marketing. What is this and how does it work? That's simple, but extremely powerful... You see, with Direct Response Marketing you are letting other things and materials do all of the selling for you... You have sales letters, brochures, T.V. or Radio Commercials, Web-Sites, etc. that do all of the selling for you. These materials do all of the selling, influencing, and persuading for you while you sit back and collect all of the cash!

Direct Response Marketing is the golden secret that we used to go from $300.00 to over $100,000,000.00 cash in less than 18 years... And many other people make our rags-to-riches story seem pale by comparison. In fact, there are many people who became instant millionaires with this powerful form of marketing. You can, too! There are plenty of books you can read, tapes you can listen to, and seminars you can attend to discover more about this powerful wealth-making formula for turning small sums of money into a huge fortune.

This powerful marketing method is the secret behind our '$100,000 A MONTH SYSTEM!' We are helping all of our Clients make money with the greatest Direct-Response Marketing secrets that we have used to sell over $100,000,000.00 worth of products and services by mail... Best of all, we do everything for our Clients! This lets them make huge profits from all of the sales, without doing any personal selling. In fact, they never have to talk to a single person! You will have the same advantage whenever you use Direct Response Marketing to do all of the selling for you.

■ **MILLIONAIRE SECRET #3**

How To Gain An Unfair Advantage Over <u>All</u> Of The People Who Are Already Making Tens Of Thousands Of Dollars A Month!

Remember, the secret to getting rich is very simple: All you have to do is find out what other people are doing to make all of their money... Then you duplicate what they're doing right and eliminate what they're doing wrong. Remember, this is how we discovered our '$100,000 A MONTH SYSTEM!' We simply found a group of people who were already making many thousands of dollars a month... Then we identified the major mistakes that they were making and added our proven Direct Response Marketing methods... and presto!

Adding Direct Response Marketing methods in place of personal selling is brilliant! **This is the golden secret that gives you an almost unfair advantage over all of the other people who are forced to put up with all of the headaches and hassles of personal selling.** Listen closely, there are plenty of people who are already making a fortune every month with the opportunity behind this new discovery. But these people are forced to go through all kinds of terrible problems that YOU will not have when you're using Direct Response Marketing to do the selling for you.

■ **MILLIONAIRE SECRET #4**

How To Get Paid Tens Of Thousands Of Dollars For Each Sale That We Make For You!

The company behind this wealth-making opportunity has developed some innovative, high-profit products that <u>millions</u> of people want and desperately need. As you'll see, the sale of these products can lead to many thousands of dollars in your pocket! It takes a little time to fully understand how this works, but here's what you must know right now: **When you're using our '$100,000 A MONTH SYSTEM!' we can make all of the sales for you!** Here are the basics: after an initial qualification period (which we all must go through) you will be eligible to get paid the full commissions on all of the sales that we make for you... If you want to do all of the selling yourself, you will keep the full amount... However, with our system, we can make ALL of the sales for you for only a 10% fee! And the sales that we make for you is just the beginning of all of the money that you can make! You see, you can also get paid on the select sales that we make for all of the people on your team! This gives you the potential power to get paid up to tens of thousands of dollars for just one initial sale that we make for you!

How To Become A Millionaire In No Time Flat!

To get rich, you must get involved in the right opportunity that's fresh and new. It must be timely and super exciting! PLUS, it must be part of an emerging trend or trends that are making many other average people a fortune right <u>now</u>! ***Just catch these opportunities at the right time, in the right way, with the right people, and you can get rich in almost no time flat!*** It sounds simple, but becoming an instant millionaire really is this easy! I know. I have made millions of dollars by finding the <u>right</u> opportunity at the <u>right</u> time and getting into it with the <u>right</u> people in the <u>right</u> way. ***<u>NOW</u> <u>YOU</u> <u>CAN</u> <u>DO</u> <u>THIS,</u> <u>TOO</u>!*** Our $100,000.00 A MONTH SYSTEM lets you cash in on 3 emerging multi-billion dollar markets in a whole new and exciting way! These trends are big now and only getting bigger! In fact, the future is so bright you gotta wear shades!

■ MILLIONAIRE SECRET #6

Why You Can Sit Back And Quickly And Easily Make Tens Of Thousands Of Dollars A Month Super Fast!

Our '$100,000 A MONTH SYSTEM!' is a powerful variation of a <u>proven</u> wealth generator that's making some people $50,000.00 to $100,000.00 a month right now in spite of the fact that they're making some very serious mistakes.

Yes, many of the people who are involved in this opportunity RIGHT NOW are getting paid more money than most doctors and lawyers make, in spite of making these huge mistakes!

This Lets YOU Tap Into A Major Wealth Formula!

The most expensive marketing expert in the world says... *"The secret to getting rich is to discover an opportunity that others are using to get rich RIGHT NOW — in spite of the serious mistakes you know they're making!"* This is the secret you'll tap into by getting involved in our new '$100,000 A MONTH SYSTEM!' We have <u>eliminated</u> all 3 mistakes that others are making, in spite of the fact that they're getting paid tens of thousands of dollars a month! There are no guarantees as to how much money you will make, but we believe that many of our Clients will use our $100,000.00 A MONTH SYSTEM to get paid over $100,000.00 a month! You could be one of them!

Finding a proven way to make money that is already making many people rich in spite of the glaring mistakes you see them making is the key to getting very rich in a hurry! Remember this! Our new discovery is already making many people tens of thousands of dollars right away... Now we have simply corrected all of the major mistakes that they're making... This gives you a major advantage over them! It also lets you duplicate their success — without dealing with all of the headaches and hassles that they are forced to go through!

> ■ ...You can't go wrong if you think of the first two minutes of your speech as an audition. It's a 120-second sample that has to convince your listeners that the remaining twenty minutes are worth their time and attention.
>
> *Roy Orben*

■ **MILLIONAIRE SECRET #7**

The #1 Reason You Can Make Thousands Of Dollars A Day Within A Few Weeks!

Our System has been built from the ground floor to pay you huge sums of daily cash that comes to you super fast! This is THE EXACT OPPOSITE of the amount of money you can make with most of the business opportunities that we research on a daily basis... You see, most opportunities only pay tiny amounts of money that come to you very slowly. It takes <u>forever</u> to get paid! This is one reason many people go broke. They simply don't make enough money fast enough... They become discouraged and quit.

But our $100,000.00 A MONTH SYSTEM is different.

This amazing discovery is designed to pay you huge sums of money very quickly! You can get paid giant sums of cash as often as every week!

<u>Here's why this has the power to make you many thousands of dollars within a few short weeks:</u>

- You are paid HUGE SUMS OF MONEY for all of the sales that we make for you!

- You'll do <u>zero</u> personal selling!

- Our system does all of the selling while you get paid the largest amount of cash!

This is designed to let you get paid the <u>maximum</u> amount of cash in the <u>minimum</u> time – with the <u>least</u> amount of effort! Many people are already making huge sums of money super fast! And our '$100,000 A MONTH SYSTEM!' makes this opportunity even more powerful for you!

■ MILLIONAIRE SECRET #8

Why We Help You Get Rich!

Most opportunities force you to do everything on your own... They take your money, give you a great-sounding business plan, and send you off on your own.

Now you must figure everything out for yourself.

It's like throwing a 5,000 piece jigsaw puzzle on the floor and expecting <u>you</u> to put it all together. You must figure everything out on your own. It is frustrating and confusing. And to make matters even worse – most opportunities have many missing pieces!

Yes, most business opportunities are similar to a 5,000 piece jigsaw puzzle with 1,789 pieces missing!

Is it any wonder why most people fail?

No!

But you won't have this problem...

Remember, we make our biggest profits by doing everything we can to help you make the largest amount of money in the fastest time – with the least amount of effort! **It is in our best interest to see to it that you get paid the largest sum of money right away!** We will do everything that we can to help you make a fast fortune.

You will be a valuable member of our team. Our success is tied to your success! ***BUT THAT'S NOT ALL: WE CAN DO EVERYTHING FOR YOU – IF YOU CHOOSE.*** That's right! You will use the same suppliers and experts that we use to build and run our multi-million dollar company!

■ MILLIONAIRE SECRET #9

How To Make Tens Of Thousands Of Dollars A Month... *In As Little As 10 Minutes A Day!*

Our '$100,000 A MONTH SYSTEM!' is a powerful and totally proven way to make huge sums of money by eliminating all three of these deadly mistakes that all of the other people who know about this secret are making!

This lets you cash-in with the secret of the richest people! **In fact, the Greek shipping billionaire, Aristotle Onassis, said:**

> *"The secret to getting wealthy is to know something that nobody else knows."*

He was right! And this is exactly what we have done...

We have taken the crème de la crème of our greatest

millionaire-making secrets that we have discovered since 1988 and reduced them to a very simple system that you can do in as little as 10 minutes a day.

Yes, all it takes is as little as 10 minutes a day to cash-in with our proven millionaire-making system! Remember, with our Direct Response Marketing methods you are letting other things and materials do all of the selling for you... Add this to the fact that you will receive (after an initial qualification period) up to thousands of dollars for every sale that we make for you and you can see why it's more than possible for you to make a fortune in as little as a few minutes a day!

Remember, you can do everything by yourself. Or we can do everything for you! This gives you the ultimate advantage over all of the other people who are already getting paid many thousands of dollars!

You will have an unfair advantage over all of these people!

And to top it off: The millionaire-making system we have developed can only be used by you and the group of others that we bring into this opportunity! The more you know about this, the more excited you'll be!

■ MILLIONAIRE SECRET #10

How To Get Thousands Of Dollars In As Little As 7 Days!

Most business opportunities pay small sums of money over a slow period of time. How slow? Well, some popular business plans tell you not to expect a profit for 3 to 5 years!

Who wants to wait 3 to 5 years to make a profit?

Not me. I'm sure you don't either!

What you need is a plan that's designed to pay you the largest amount of money – in the fastest time – with the least amount of headaches and hassles! **And this is _exactly_ what our $100,000.00 A MONTH SYSTEM is designed to do for you!**

This System is designed to let you get paid thousands of dollars within <u>days</u> from the time our System goes to work for you!

This is not a guarantee or promise that you will make thousands of dollars within days – but others have – and you can, too!

One thing is certain: You will be shocked and amazed when you discover how our $100,000.00 A MONTH SYSTEM is designed to pay you many thousands of dollars in the fastest time!

- You can get paid thousands of dollars within days!

- You will have our easy system that's so simple that a 12-year-old child can understand and use it.

- We will be there for you – to do all that we can to see to it that you get paid the largest amount of money in the shortest period of time!

Most people are wasting their precious time and energy by trying to make money with opportunities that will <u>never</u> make them rich.

But you can't make this mistake. Here's something you must know...

Life is too short to work hard and then "hope" you will make big money "someday"...

Life is too short to get involved in opportunities that force you to wait by the mailbox every month for a check.

- You must get paid first!

- You must get paid the largest sum of money and not the company behind the opportunity.

- You must be able to make thousands of dollars in the fastest time.

AND NOW YOU HAVE ALL OF THESE THINGS AND MORE!

IT'S ALL RIGHT HERE IN THIS $100,000.00 A MONTH SYSTEM!

How fast can you get paid?

Nobody can say for sure, but...

I MADE $10,000.00 MY FIRST WEEK!

Yes, I made ten thousand dollars in my first week – before I knew what I was doing!

Think about that. How many opportunities can put $10,000.00 cash in your pocket in the first week? None! But this one can! I am proof that this can make you huge sums of fast cash!

■ **MILLIONAIRE SECRET #11**

How To Get Rich In Total Privacy!

Most opportunities are not private. You must meet and talk to many people every day. You are exposed. You can't do anything in your business without everyone knowing about it.

In fact, with most opportunities you must let everyone know what you're doing or you won't make any money. You must approach everyone you meet and try to get them to buy from you. Your life is filled with many people who know everything you're doing. You must meet with all of these people and try to get them to do business with you. YOU HAVE NO PRIVACY. There is no escape from all of the pressures that are closing in on you...

This is how 95% of all business people are forced to live...

But you won't have any of these headaches and hassles with our $100,000.00 A MONTH SYSTEM! You'll make money in total privacy!

With our System, nobody will know what you're doing to make all of your money! You will be totally free:

- You will <u>never</u> talk with anyone...

- You will <u>never</u> personally sell anything to anyone!

- You will be in the powerful position that 99% of all other people can only dream of!

If the ability to make money in total privacy were the only advantage of our wealth-making discovery, it would be one of the greatest ways to stay home and make money. <u>But wait, there's more!</u>

For starters...

You can do everything in as little as 10 minutes a day!

Most business people work way too hard for too little money. They spend many years putting in long hours with endless frustrations. They end up quitting and become bitter and angry.

I run into people all of the time who used to be in business and now regret every minute of it. They're filled with anger because all of their dreams of becoming financially free have been crushed...

■ Self-employed people make up less than 20 percent of the workers in America but account for two-thirds of the millionaires.

Dr. Thomas Stanley and Dr. William Danko
"The Millionaire Next Door"

■ Keep away from people who try to belittle your ambitions. Small people always do that , but the really great let you know that you, too, can become great.

Mark Twain

<u>But I've also seen</u>...

MANY AVERAGE PEOPLE BECOME MILLIONAIRES!

I've been a business opportunity investigator and researcher since 1988 and have met many average people who are making more money than most doctors and lawyers can only dream of!

These people are getting rich because they stumbled onto the right opportunity at the right time! Now they're making many hundreds of thousands and even millions of dollars! But, even more importantly − many of these people are getting rich with very little time or effort! Yes, as amazing as it may sound − it's the absolute truth! In fact...

Whoever said "It's impossible to get rich quick" <u>WAS WRONG!</u>

I have met many people who started with little or even nothing and became millionaires in a few short years!

The secret to getting very rich with little time and effort is simple: **All you need are the right systems in place.** These systems take time to build − but once they're built − you can kick back and let them make money for you.

IT SOUNDS TOO GOOD TO BE TRUE AND YET IT IS TRUE.

The world's richest people have many systems in place that make them huge sums of wealth! These people can be shopping, sleeping, or on vacation while their "systems" do all of the work for them! *<u>Now this same advantage will be working for you!</u>*

You can cash-in with the powerful $100,000.00 A MONTH SYSTEM that we have built for you! **We have worked very hard to build this system for you... Now it's ready to go!** You'll be cashing-in with the same system that we're using to reach our goal of making millions of dollars with this amazing discovery!

3 Simple Things You Need To Make Millions Of Dollars...
Best Of All — We Give You All Three!

Many people <u>never</u> get rich because they don't have the right help from the right people. This is especially true when you're first getting started. You must find experts who know how to turn small sums of money into a huge fortune in the fastest time.

Just find the right people who help you use the right opportunity and you can get rich fast! *This was the #1 secret to our rags-to-riches success.* **It made us millions of dollars very quickly. IT CAN MAKE <u>YOU</u> A FORTUNE, TOO!**

Listen closely. My wife, Eileen, and I had a lot of help support, and guidance from millionaire-making experts such as Russ von Hoelscher and Dan Kennedy. **Thanks to the help Russ von Hoelscher gave us, we made almost $10,000,000.00 in our first four years!** And thanks to other experts such as Dan Kennedy, Alan R. Bechtold, Jeff Gardner, Eric Bechtold, Chris Lakey, and many others, we've brought in over $100-MILLION DOLLARS so far!

<u>Please</u> <u>don't</u> <u>think</u> <u>I'm</u> <u>bragging</u> <u>about</u> <u>all</u> <u>our</u> <u>wealth</u>. <u>I'm</u> <u>not</u>. But I am bragging on the fact that having the right help, support, and guidance from the right people has made us multi-millionaires, starting from scratch. It can make a fortune for <u>you</u>, too!

In fact, all you need are 3 things to get rich:

1. An opportunity that's making a fortune for other average people.

2. The right help, support, and guidance from experts who have already made a great deal of money for other people.

3. A marketing system that does <u>all</u> of the work for you.

When you have all three of these things, **the question is not;** *"Will you get rich?"* **OH, NO! The only question will be,** *"When will you get rich and how rich will you get?"* **BECAUSE YOU WILL GET RICH!**

In fact...

It's only a matter of how much money you'll make and how fast it will come RUSHING to you!

Remember, this proven opportunity is already making many average people tens of thousands of dollars a month! **And you'll get the same system that we're using to achieve our goal of making millions with this all-new wealth-making discovery. PLUS, WE CAN DO EVERYTHING FOR YOU!**

■ **MILLIONAIRE SECRET #13**

Why We Really Can Do Everything For You!

Although there is quite a buzz on the Internet about this amazing wealth discovery, it's still brand new! **Tens of millions of people have never heard of this! And now we have a proven way to reach this huge group of hot prospects!** There's no room to go into the details right now... *However, I will say this:* one of the ways you'll cash in with this lucrative wealth-making discovery is through our proven system that lets you reach the people who are searching for a proven way to make money.

THIS ONE SECRET ALONE could make you very rich!

Listen closely. I have made the bulk of my fortune by serving this very lucrative marketplace called: *"the opportunity market."* This is a market of tens of millions of people who are desperately searching for the ultimate way to become financially independent.

This giant and highly lucrative market is one of the three multi-billion dollar markets that have been combined to create our revolutionary $100,000.00 A MONTH SYSTEM!

Our System lets you tap into this market the easy way...

You will never have to speak to anyone – unless you want. You will never do any personal selling or have to convince anyone of anything. Our system does all of this for you!

You will use our System to tap into this very lucrative marketplace. **This is one of the most exciting secrets in our $100,000.00 A MONTH SYSTEM!**

Why? Because I will reveal the little-known tips, tricks, and strategies that we have used to make millions in this booming market. Best of all, we have put all of our secrets into this revolutionary new $100,000.00 A MONTH SYSTEM!

This lets you cash-in with the secrets that have brought us a total of over $100-million dollars in our first 18 years!

You will be so thrilled when you discover the amazing wealth secrets that let you tap into the opportunity market! Remember, we are experts at reaching and serving this highly lucrative marketplace. **And all of our greatest secrets have gone into this amazing $100,000.00 A MONTH SYSTEM!** If this were the only thing you were receiving, it would be the greatest wealth-maker ever! But there's still more! In fact, the final way this is designed to make you rich will take several pages to reveal to you!

■ MILLIONAIRE SECRET #14

Why Many Very Smart People Go Broke And How To Easily Avoid It.

Many new opportunities are too new! The market for the products and services that are sold has not been established enough. They are too far ahead of the curve. Many smart people are visionaries who 'see the future' and jump into these opportunities way too soon. Because of this, they end up going broke in a hurry.

CONSIDER THIS: the only people who can get rich with these opportunities are the Fortune 500 companies who have a limitless amount of money to spend. What you must do is let these giant corporations spend the billions of dollars necessary to develop these revolutionary new markets for the latest cutting-edge products and services...

Then, when the market is established and already bringing in many billions of dollars, there is room for the rest of us to come in and make many millions of easy dollars.

Remember, many of the pioneers got scalped! Opportunities that are too new are also very risky. You must let others pave the way for you. You sit back, watch for all of the emerging multi-billion dollar markets and opportunities, and then you make sure you are among the <u>first</u> to get in! **When you do this the right way with the right opportunities – you can become a multi-millionaire in no time flat!**

<u>And this is good news for you</u>!

Why? Because our $100,000.00 A MONTH SYSTEM is the greatest discovery ever for cashing in with three multi-billion dollar markets that are already generating a fortune and getting ready to explode with growth! **These three markets are hot <u>now</u> and only getting hotter!** The timing is perfect for this amazing opportunity!

■ MILLIONAIRE SECRET #15

Here's Your Golden Key To Getting Thousands Of Dollars In As Little As 10 Days!

The people who use these plans and programs almost <u>never</u> make any serious money. Only the promoters get rich. The average person doesn't stand a chance of making any serious money with most opportunities. This is so sad. These opportunities are just <u>not</u> built for the average person who has very little time, money, experience, or contacts. Only the heavy hitters get rich. Only the guys and gals who have a fortune to spend or have a lot of powerful contacts and connections...

■ Advertisements are now so numerous that they are very negligently perused and it has therefore become necessary to gain attention by magnificence of promises and by eloquence, sometimes sublime and sometimes pathetic. Promise — large promise — is the soul of advertising.

Samuel Johnson 1759

But our $100,000.00 A MONTH SYSTEM is totally different!

Here's why:

Our $100,000.00 A MONTH SYSTEM is designed from the ground up to put the <u>largest</u> amount of money into your pocket in the fastest period of time, with the least amount of effort! Because of this, many average people are making thousands of dollars a month right away! This Is YOUR GOLDEN KEY to getting thousands of dollars in as little as 10 days!

Yes, many people with little or no business knowledge or skills – or very little time or money – are experiencing FAST success right out of the gate!

But wait. There's more!

You see, this $100,000.00 A MONTH SYSTEM is also designed to reward <u>me</u> in the most powerful and direct way possible to do everything within my power to make sure that <u>you</u> <u>do</u> <u>make</u> the largest amount of money in the fastest time! I am rewarded greatly to do all I can to help you get off to a powerful and profitable start!

The <u>more</u> I can do to help you make money right away – the more money I personally make! This is brilliant!

If <u>this</u> one advantage was the only thing that separated this opportunity from all the others – it would be enough for you to throw your whole heart and soul into our $100,000.00 A MONTH SYSTEM!

3 Simple Questions That Can Save You Many Thousands Of Dollars.

Many new opportunities violate certain laws or ethics.

You may get rich – but who wants to go to jail?

And who wants to be involved in anything immoral? Not me. I'm sure YOU don't either. And what good is it to get rich if you have to take advantage of others to make all of your money?

Here is a strange situation that we have noticed over the years: Many times the "hottest" opportunities that are most exciting were also the ones with the biggest problems.

It's interesting to note that...

Many of the opportunities that are _most_ exciting are nothing but hype and hot air! There is no foundation under them that can make you rich.

We look at these flash-in-the-pan opportunities that promise to _"make you a millionaire in the next 30 days"_ and ask...

■ Where's the product or service behind all of this?

■ Where is the market for this 'red-hot, newfangled gizmo' that's going to take the world by storm?

And the final question:

■ Would it be possible to make millions of dollars _without_ all of the buzz that's created by the emotional believers who are hyping it up?

If the answer to that question is "NO!" then grab your wallet and run as fast as you can!

Listen closely. The more you look at most of the hottest

opportunities that are sweeping the nation, the more you'll see that it is nothing more than hype that's fueling the whole thing.

HERE'S THE RULE OF THUMB: The more hype there is behind any opportunity, the more illegal or immoral it tends to be. There are exceptions, but this is a general rule for you to consider.

■ MILLIONAIRE SECRET #17

Why Average People Are Making As Much As $50,000.00 to $100,000.00 A Month!

Our $100,000.00 A MONTH SYSTEM is a powerful combination of 3 multi-billion dollar markets that are already producing hundreds of billions of dollars a year. And these three markets are growing by leaps and bounds! This is the #1 reason why average people are making as much as $50,000.00 to $100,000.00 a month right now!

I have personally made millions of dollars in two of these three exploding markets that are part of our '$100,000 A MONTH SYSTEM!' and I have barely scratched the surface of all of the money that any average person can make! **There are literally billions of dollars on the table just waiting to be made!** And you will be tapping into this enormous wealth!

Long-Term Cash Is Waiting For You!

Many of the new opportunities that we look at are flash-in-the-pan schemes – built on pure hype.

When the hype runs out, they're gone forever.

Please listen to me...

I have seen so many different opportunities come and go – it makes me sick to think about it. Every year there are two or three really hot opportunities that sweep the nation. They are like a giant forest fire that consumes tens of thousands of acres of beautiful trees. Only, in this case, it's the people who get burned.

I have met so many people whose lives are ruined because they got involved in some exciting opportunity that was burning through the nation like a raging forest fire. These people end up losing their money. But they also lose their self-respect and their enthusiasm for making a lot of money and having all of the wonderful things that could and should be theirs.

They become totally defeated and are never able to bounce back.

They give up on their dreams.

They become bitter and cynical.

But the major reason <u>why</u> these "red-hot opportunities" are here today and gone tomorrow is because there is nothing <u>solid</u> behind them.

Once you get past the hype and B.S. there's nothing else behind it. There is no "real" product or service. There is no "real" market other than all of the people who are promoting the whole thing. Without the buzz of these highly emotional believers – the whole thing would <u>never</u> make a dollar for anyone! And that's what happens! When the hype runs out – there's no market left!

But again, our $100,000.00 A MONTH SYSTEM is totally different...

HERE'S WHY:

- Our $100.000.00 A MONTH SYSTEM is built on solid products with very-high perceived values.

- These products are all part of a multi-billion dollar marketplace that is growing by leaps and bounds!

- The products are unique. They deliver tremendous value, but thanks to the miracle of technology – your actual costs to distribute these items is very low.

Because of these 3 things, your profits soar!

These three ingredients are your foundation to wealth! And this is the powerful foundation behind our $100,000.00 A MONTH SYSTEM! This gives you the same powerful advantages that other people are using RIGHT NOW to bring in as much as $50,000 to $100,000 a month and even more!

■ MILLIONAIRE SECRET #18

The 'ONE TRILLION DOLLARS A YEAR WEALTH SECRET!'

Our '$100,000 A MONTH SYSTEM!' is similar to a high-dollar franchise! How? That's simple, but amazingly powerful. You see, a franchise does everything that they can to make sure that each one of its location owners brings in the largest sum of money! This makes huge sums of money for both of them. How much money? That's the shocking part... You see, the franchise industry brings in *ONE TRILLION DOLLARS A YEAR!*

The reason this industry brings in one trillion dollars a year is because the parent company does everything that they can to help their individual franchisees make the largest sums of money... **Now you will have this same type of wealth-making power working for you!**

Most opportunities have no way to help you make huge sums of money.

Most opportunities leave you out in the cold... They give you great ideas for making money and then force you to do everything on your own... There's nobody to call. There are no support services to fall back on. You must face many obstacles on your path to getting started – and there's nobody to help you get through them...

Is it any wonder why most people fail?

But our $100,000.00 A MONTH SYSTEM is different because...

We will not let you fail!

With this amazing System – we are there for you every step of the way. Remember, we earn our biggest profits by helping you get off to a powerful start. **The more we can do to help you make the most money, in the fastest time, with the least effort, the more money we make!**

THIS GIVES US THE _ULTIMATE_ INCENTIVE TO HELP YOU GET OFF TO A POWERFUL START AND MAKE THE MAXIMUM SUM OF FAST CASH!

THIS IS SO GREAT, I MUST SAY IT AGAIN: The more we can do to help you make fast money – the more money we will make for ourselves!

This is the ultimate way that I can do everything within my power to help you get rich and put large sums of cash in my pocket!

It's the PERFECT win-win situation for you and me! This gives you the greatest way to cash in with 'THE ONE TRILLION DOLLAR WEALTH SECRET!'

■ MILLIONAIRE SECRET #19

Why You <u>Never</u> Have To Worry About Getting Cheated.

So many people have lost their dreams of getting rich because of some fly-by-night company that took their money and ran...

This is a major problem. It is especially true with multi-level marketing companies.

In fact, I have seen so many multi-level companies take-the-money-and-run – <u>it makes me sick</u>.

These network marketing companies are infamous for cheating people out of their hard-earned money...

I have met so many people who lost their money and their dream of ever getting rich. <u>This breaks my heart</u>. There are so many fly-by-night companies who promote business opportunities that it's hard for the average person to tell which ones are legitimate and which ones aren't. **That's why you should be very skeptical about each new opportunity you look at.** You must protect yourself against all of the rip-off artists out there.

We Started Our Company To Help People Avoid Getting Ripped Off And Cheated

Eileen and I started our company, Mid-American Opportunity Research Enterprises, Inc. (a.k.a. M.O.R.E., Incorporated), to help our clients navigate these shark-infested waters of the business opportunity market. We have seen so many shady deals that it makes us angry and sad.

Eileen and I know what it's like to be lied to and cheated by all of the scammers and con men... We were taken advantage of many times *before* we discovered a proven way to make millions of dollars.

I have never forgot all of the pain and suffering that we went through. I sincerely hope that you are not going through this right now.

■ The way to get things done is not to mind who gets the credit for doing them.

Benjamin Jowett

■ For a man to achieve all that is demanded of him he must regard himself as greater than he is.

Johann Wolfgang von Goethe

■ Well done is better than well said.

Benjamin Franklin

■ When you reach for the stars, you may not quite get them, but you won't come up with a handful of mud either.

Leo Burnett

So it's okay if you're skeptical about <u>this</u> or any other opportunity. But don't let your skepticism turn into cynicism...

You must stay open and receptive to new things – or you may end up walking away from an opportunity that could make you millions of dollars in a few years... just like the one that made us instant millionaires.

And that brings me back to our $100,000.00 A MONTH SYSTEM...

This amazing money-making system is different and better than any other opportunity because <u>you</u> make the largest amount of money – and you get paid first! You make your money <u>before</u> the company behind this discovery gets its money! This gives you the ultimate power to get rich!

Consider the awesome power that you will have:

■ You can get large amounts of money paid to you first.

■ You can get these large amounts of cash as often as every day!

This is an amazing breakthrough because the company behind this breakthrough does <u>not</u> get paid until and unless <u>you</u> <u>and</u> <u>I</u> get paid! This is the exact opposite of how <u>most</u> opportunities work!

You will have the ultimate power!

God forbid should something ever happen to the company behind this brilliant wealth-making system. But even if this International Company would go out of business for some reason – you and I would <u>still</u> be sitting pretty because we got our money first!

There is <u>no</u> way that this company can <u>ever</u> take our money and run – because we got paid first! There would be no money for them to take! This is the one major advantage that I love more than <u>any</u> other... So will you!

The #1 Reason Why <u>Most</u> Opportunities Will <u>Never</u> Make You Rich.

Most opportunities force you to work long hours with very little pay in the beginning...

I see so many business owners who are tired, frustrated, and totally burned out. It makes me sad. All of the joy they once felt for their businesses is gone. They have been beaten down by the daily pressures... They have a defeated look in their eyes.

But here's one major fact that you <u>must</u> know right now...

Are you ready?

OKAY, here it is: Most business opportunities will <u>never</u> make you rich — no matter how many hours you put in.

Most opportunities are simply not designed to ever make you rich. The markets for the products and services are too small... The demand for what they are selling is too low. Or 1,000 other factors... This is the #1 reason why they will never make you rich, no matter what you have...

But our '$100,000 A MONTH SYSTEM!' is different...

You see, our $100,000.00 A MONTH SYSTEM <u>is</u> designed to make you super rich! It has been designed and built from the ground floor to make you the largest amount of money in the shortest time! It pays you huge sums of fast cash for very small efforts! This is the key reason why others are already getting rich!

Remember, our $100,000.00 A MONTH SYSTEM gives you many advantages that other people don't have! The more you know about this, the more excited you'll be!

The Only 3 Things You Need To Make Millions Of Dollars!

Many opportunities offer products that nobody wants.

If you want to make millions of dollars – here are the only 3 things you need:

1. The market for your products or services comes first. Others must already be making millions of dollars by selling the same types of products and services that you want to sell.

2. The products or services you offer must have unique features and advantages that set them apart from everything else. The perceived value must be very high. There must be something very exciting about them that makes people want to buy. People must be <u>thrilled</u> with the items you sell!

3. You must have a proven marketing system that automatically sells to the millions of people who want your exciting product or service!

When you have all three of these elements working in your favor... you can get very rich in a short period of time!

And this explains why most people never get rich:

■ There is a small market or even no market for the product or service being offered. And if there <u>is</u> a market for the items being sold – it's very small.

■ Most of the products and services being sold are <u>not</u> new and exciting. There is nothing about these items to stir people's souls – nothing to get people fired up and excited.

■ And there is no marketing system for selling the products or services. <u>This forces people to become salespeople</u>. And who wants to sell for a living?

But our $100,000.00 A MONTH SYSTEM is totally different! This gives you <u>all</u> three of the main things you need to get rich:

- This System combines 3 of the hottest markets that are big now and only growing bigger!

- Other people are already making many billions of dollars with products and services that are similar to the ones we offer. But our items are totally unique!

- Our proven multi-million dollar marketing system does all of the selling for you! There is no selling. You have total privacy. There's no manual labor! It's like a money-machine!

This marketing system has been proven to make tens of millions of dollars for us! <u>THAT'S WHY I BELIEVE THAT IT CAN MAKE YOU RICH, TOO!</u> This is especially true because we have added the amazing secrets behind our revolutionary new $100,000.00 A MONTH SYSTEM!

■ **MILLIONAIRE SECRET #22**

The '$8,000.00 A Day Wealth Secret!' — And How To Use It To Get Rich!

I have a friend who charges $8,000.00 a day for his consulting services. And there is so much demand for his highly specialized knowledge that people are standing in line to pay him!

Yes, people fly from around the world to Cleveland, Ohio, to see this man and feel lucky to pay him his $8,000.00 a day fee. After all, his highly specialized knowledge can make them many tens of millions of dollars. So the $8,000.00 a day fee my friend charges is a drop in the bucket for them. And it's also a drop in the bucket for him! You see, this man also has developed many specialized products and services that pay him **Millions of dollars every year.**

This is only one example, but it is illustrative of all of the people who are getting very rich because they have some very specialized products or services.

But what about the average guy or gal?

What chance do they have to get rich?

This is the burning question I ask myself on a daily basis. And the answer is simpler and easier than you can imagine!

Are you ready? Okay. Here we go...

All you have to do is have full control over a very specialized product or service that others have spent many years to develop. That's it! This is all that you do to enjoy the same advantages that the people who are making millions of dollars by selling specialized in-demand products and services enjoy!

This is the foundation behind our $100,000.00 A MONTH SYSTEM!

In other parts of this book I will be telling you about the extreme value in the specialized high-ticket items that make up the foundation of our $100,000.00 A MONTH SYSTEM. You will be very impressed! This lets you cash in with 'The $8,000 A Day Wealth Secret!' in the ultimate way! The next millionaire secret tells you why! Read on...

■ MILLIONAIRE SECRET #23

3 Reasons <u>Why</u> This Opportunity Has The Power To Make You A Millionaire In No Time Flat!

Remember, one of the hottest ways to get rich is to sell very specialized and highly in-demand information... This is <u>exactly</u> what you'll be getting when you get involved in our '$100,000 A MONTH SYSTEM!'

- Life is either a daring adventure or nothing.

    Helen Keller

- No matter what accomplishments you make, somebody helps you.

    Althea Gibson Darben

- You don't learn to hold your own in the world by standing on guard, but by attacking and getting well hammered yourself.

    George Bernard Shaw

- A man's deeds are his life.

    West African saying

Here are the three reasons why this has the power to make you millions of dollars in the fastest period of time:

- The basic items you will have control over <u>are</u> complicated.

- These items are very specialized and took a great deal of time and expertise to develop. They were developed by experienced experts who spent many years on them. But now they are finished! And now you can have full control over these items!

- This gives you all of the advantages that many of the most knowledgeable and experienced experts have – without knowing <u>anything</u> that they know! It gives you the ultimate leverage to get paid the largest amount of money in the minimum time!

Please stop and think carefully about these three main advantages... You'll see. This truly does give you the opportunity to make enormous sums of money in the shortest period of time! It's the simple, but proven formula that you can use to become a millionaire in no time flat!

How We Help You Cash In With The '2,500 Year Old Wealth Making Secret!'

You know the famous Chinese saying, *"A journey of a thousand miles starts with the first step."* And it's true! You <u>must</u> get off to a good start. This is a wealth-making secret that is even more important today than it was 2,500 years ago!

Why? That's simple. You see, most businesses are complicated and difficult to start.

In most opportunities, there are a thousand decisions to make and a thousand possible roads to travel. You are faced with so many obstacles. There are many problems and stressful decisions that must be made before you even begin.

But starting your own business does not have to be this way... This should be an exciting adventure...<u>and</u> <u>now</u> <u>it</u> <u>can</u> <u>be</u>!

OKAY, here's where it gets even more exciting!

Please listen closely...

Our $100.000.00 A MONTH SYSTEM is <u>not</u> a franchise — but it does offer many of the same advantages that you would receive if you invested in a franchise.

You see, if you invest in a franchise — they will do everything possible to help you start and run your business.

For example...

- They will give you everything you need – all of the training – all of the guidance and support.

- They have specialists who will be there for you, to make it super easy to get started!

- The franchise specialists are very experienced. They know *exactly* what to do and how to do it.

- They will be right there by your side. They'll make all of the complicated decisions that would be impossible for you to make, but are very simple for them....

- They make it easy and even fun!

With a franchise, you are in business for yourself, but <u>never</u> by yourself. <u>You are part of a successful team</u>. You have all of the help, support, and guidance that you need, every step of the way. This makes it easy to get off to the most powerful and profitable start!

When you invest in a franchise you're <u>never</u> alone. You will have the security of always knowing that there will be many experts waiting to help you whenever you need it. This can mean all of the difference between a major success and a total failure.

This is the biggest reason why tens of thousands of people invest their entire net worth to buy a successful franchise. *<u>They know that having the proven track record behind the opportunity, and all of the help and support,</u> is their golden ticket to becoming financially independent for life!*

And now <u>you</u> will have this same powerful wealth-making advantage working for <u>you</u>!

Here's how:

Our amazing new $100,000.00 A MONTH SYSTEM gives you many of the same advantages that a high-dollar franchise gives you, <u>without</u> investing hundreds of thousands of dollars.

With this new System, you'll be in business for yourself, but <u>never</u> by yourself. We will be there for you, to do all that we can to see to it that you make the largest sum of money in the fastest time!

After all, **the more money we can help you deposit into your bank account — the more money we make.** This gives us the ultimate reward to do all that we can to help you get rich!

■ **MILLIONAIRE SECRET #25**

How To Gain An Unfair Advantage Over All Of Your Competitors!

There is nothing uniquely different about most opportunities that gets people fired up! The products and services are as boring as dirt! The markets they serve are not growing quickly enough or – if they are involved in a marketplace that <u>is</u> growing – there is <u>nothing</u> about the company or its products and services to make it stand out.

But you won't have this major problem.

You see, when what you offer is totally unique, it stands out head and shoulders over everything else. And when you do this right – there is <u>no</u> competition! Sure, you will always have competitors. But you'll never have any real competition!

This one secret gives you an unfair advantage over everyone else! And this is the most powerful thing about our revolutionary new $100,000.00 A MONTH SYSTEM! This gives you an instant unfair advantage over all of the other competitors who are cashing in with the basic secrets in this System right now!

This is totally unique from every other opportunity on the market! It eliminates all of the problems that are built into all of the other opportunities that I research on a daily basis. It's truly unique in every way!

Now consider this: One of the markets our $100,000.00 A MONTH SYSTEM serves is the opportunity market...

This is the market that has made me and my wife many millions of dollars – even though we started with almost no money. And, in this one market alone, our $100,000.00 A MONTH SYSTEM shines brightly!

<u>No</u> <u>other</u> <u>opportunity</u> <u>can</u> <u>touch</u> <u>this</u>! It is totally fresh, new, and exciting! It solves <u>all</u> of the problems we see that are built into all of the other opportunities.

■ MILLIONAIRE SECRET #26

The ABC Formula For Making Massive Amounts Of Money In The Minimum Time!

Being an opportunity investigator is a full-time job! There's <u>never</u> a shortage of opportunities out there too look at. Most "claim" to be different. But they're not. They are the same old plans and programs that parade themselves as being new.

It takes us about 30 seconds to spot these phony rip-off opportunities. In fact, we can usually spot them from a mile away.

It's so easy to become cynical when you study one opportunity after another and keep finding the same old worn out scams and schemes... After a while you become even more skeptical and angry about all of the hype and B.S. out there.

But every once in a while I get fooled!

Every once in a great while I run into an opportunity that looks too good to be true. But then I find out that it is true! And that's what happened with our $100,000.00 A MONTH SYSTEM!

I had many doubts when I first saw this opportunity. I thought it seemed too good to be true. *"There has to be something I'm missing here,"* I kept saying to myself. But the harder I studied this opportunity, the more I knew that ***this is the rare diamond!***

But I don't expect you to take my word for it... So here are a few of the things I look at when examining an opportunity.

Here are the main questions I ask when I want to separate the few opportunities that can make you rich from all of the plans and programs that never make you a dime:

- Is there a large and growing market for the products and services being offered?

- Is there something unique about the company or its products that sets it apart from all of the others?

- Is there a marketing system that does some or all of the selling?

If the answer to these three questions is "No" or negative in any way – then I stop. So should you!

And I am so proud to tell you that our $100,000.00 A MONTH SYSTEM has passed all of my hardest tests with flying colors!

This really is the perfect way to make large sums of money in the fastest time! Here's the A-B-C Formula behind this System that is designed to make you the maximum sum of money in the minimum amount of time:

A. **The market for all of the items being offered is huge!** These markets are big and lucrative right now – and growing by leaps and bounds! Many people are already getting rich – and the best years are still ahead!

B. **The International Company that developed this powerful opportunity is truly unique!** This company is a genuine breath of fresh air – especially when you compare it with all of the other companies in the marketplace.

C. **Our marketing system does <u>all</u> of the selling for you!** This is designed to pay you big money without talking to anyone!

It does take a couple of days to fully understand every aspect of this opportunity, but once you do – you will be more excited than you have ever been in your entire life!

The #1 Secret That Lets The Rich Keep Getting Even Richer — And How <u>You</u> Can Cash-In With This Secret Now!

The richest people in the world spend a great deal of time looking for the <u>next</u> <u>big</u> <u>thing</u>. They are searching for major trends that are getting ready to explode!

These wealthy people have well-trained analysts who scan the globe for the next hottest opportunity. They spot these things. Then they jump in with both feet — before everyone else! They make GIANT sums of money because they get in at the right time. This is the #1 reason why the rich keep getting even richer — and how you can cash in with this secret... starting now!

■ Have the courage to act instead of react.

Earlene Larson Jenks

■ The only difference between a rut and a grave is their dimensions.

Ellen Glasgow

■ A horse never runs so fast as when he has other horses to catch up and outpace.

Ovid

And that brings me to a great metaphor...

Getting rich is a lot like surfing... You must catch the waves the right way at the right time. You get in front of the right wave and you can ride it all the way!

Remember, timing is everything. When you study the lives of the people who make the largest sums of money, you will always see that they got involved in the right opportunity at the right time.

They caught the wave when it was small and rode it in for major wealth! They put themselves in a powerful position to make the largest sum of money in the fastest time!

The power of momentum carries them to wealth like a giant wave carries the professional surfer! YOU CAN DO THIS, TOO... All you have to do is know how to spot these giant waves and then catch them at the right time. That's it! Do it right and you can make money in a faster period of time than you have <u>ever</u> dreamed of making! The money will come rushing in so fast that it will seem like a dream! Go onto the next millionaire secret and I'll show you how...

■ MILLIONAIRE SECRET #28

The Secret That Made Us Over $10-MILLION DOLLARS In Our First Four Years — And How We Built It Into Our '$100,000.00 A MONTH SYSTEM!'

My wife and I have caught the wave just right several times over the years and had millions of dollars come rushing in so fast that we couldn't believe it! Now I want the same thing to happen to you!

Consider this...

When you catch the wealth-making wave just right — it can make you so much money, so fast, that you will be shocked!

The first time this happened to us — we brought in over $10,000,000.00 in our first four years... It was like a raging river of money that flowed into our lives so fast that we couldn't believe it! The same thing can happen to you! All you need to do is catch the right opportunity, at the right time, in the right way. This is the secret that made us instant millionaires... It can do the same thing for you! And that's good news for you because... **Our $100,000.00 A MONTH SYSTEM is a high-powered opportunity that is getting ready to explode! Best of all, this lets you cash in with the same secret that brought us so many millions of**

dollars, so quickly, that we had to pinch ourselves to make sure that it was really happening! I can't wait to show you how this powerful discovery combines three very exciting billion dollar markets that are growing quickly!

■ MILLIONAIRE SECRET #29

How To <u>Instantly</u> Spot The Opportunities That Can Make You A Millionaire In No Time Flat From <u>All</u> The Others!

To get rich, you must find a business that is already making other average people very rich. You simply find out what these people are doing to make all of their money – then duplicate their actions. It's so simple!

You really can get rich by finding out how others are doing it – and then duplicating their actions!

But most business people <u>never</u> do this. The businesses they chose to get into were picked with very little awareness. They <u>never stop</u> to realize that the businesses they are in will <u>never</u> make them rich.

I run into former businesspeople all the time who say things like, "Thank God, I'm out of that!" **They meet me and assume that my life in business is a living nightmare like theirs was.**

But nothing could be further from the truth!

After many years of struggle, my wife and I finally discovered the perfect business that ended up making us millions of dollars – and has provided us with all of the best that life has to offer! It has been a major struggle – but it has been more than worth it!

Now I want <u>you</u> to experience the thrill of having the perfect home-based business! Please remember – there are many people who are already making as much as $50,000.00 to $100,000.00 a month with the basic secrets in our $100,000.00 A MONTH SYSTEM!

All you have to do is discover what they are doing and then duplicate their exact steps. We will show you how to do it! This is the simple and easy way that you can instantly spot the best opportunities that can make you a millionaire in no time flat!

■ MILLIONAIRE SECRET #30

5 Rock-Solid Reasons <u>Why</u> Our '$100,000.00 A MONTH SYSTEM!' Discovery Is At Least 1,000,000 Times More Powerful Than Most Multi-Level Or Network Marketing Opportunities!

With most opportunities, you get paid small sums of money. You are forced to sell low-ticket items with very little profit margin. And to make matters even worse – you have to put in a great deal of time and work – and then wait around to get paid.

And if all of this is not bad enough – there's one final nail in the coffin... It's the simple fact that...

Many business opportunities are infamous for never paying you all of the money that they owe you.

The best examples of the companies who cheat you out of your money are the different multi-level marketing companies that come and go every year... Some of these companies are red-hot for a few months or years. A few of the folks who get in *first* make a lot of money. But most of the time, the <u>only</u> people who get rich are the ones who start these companies or the highly gifted salespeople we call *"heavy-hitters."*

That's why I say...

My best advice for you is to stay away from traditional multi-level or network marketing companies. A few of these companies are exceptional – <u>but</u> <u>most</u> <u>are</u> <u>not</u>. They will end up taking your money and leaving you angry and bitter.

I have been so frustrated over the years with all of the multi-level companies who promise so much and deliver so little. I have a genuine love and hate relationship with <u>all</u> of these opportunities.

I love MLM because their idea of "people-helping-people" is brilliant! And I got my start in business by joining all kinds of multi-level marketing companies. **In fact, if it weren't for these types of companies – I would <u>not</u> be a millionaire today.** You see, it was all the great people that I met in these MLM meetings and pep rallies who helped me believe that I really could become a millionaire...

But, in the early years, I never made a dime in MLM...

And along the way I grew to hate multi-level marketing. In fact, <u>*I hate it with a vengeance*</u>.

I have met so many wonderful people whose lives were shattered because the multi-level marketing company they worked so hard to build went out of business... Or worse, **some of these companies were started by criminals who let their distributors build them so they could take the money and run...** This makes me sick to my stomach...

And, in 1999 I became so angry, I wrote my famous book:

"MLM Sucks!"

This book goes into great detail about <u>all</u> of the reasons that MLM is a terrible way to make money.

But this is just one more way that our $100,000.00 A MONTH SYSTEM shines so very brightly! This powerful new system gives you some of the <u>greatest</u> <u>benefits</u> of network marketing – <u>without</u> any of the terrible side effects!

Here Are 5 Rock-Solid Reasons <u>Why</u> Our '$100,000.00 A MONTH SYSTEM!' Discovery Is At Least 1,000,000 Times More Powerful Than Most Multi-Level Or Network Marketing Opportunities:

1. You get the largest sum of money paid directly to you!

2. You get paid first – before the company gets paid.

3. You have <u>all</u> kinds of help, every step of the way.

4. And you have the ability to get paid large sums of daily cash while building a growing and dependable monthly income that can keep growing bigger and never stop!

5. And last, but not least... God forbid, **but if something should ever happen to the International Company behind this wealth-making breakthrough, you will still be in great shape financially!** After all, you were and will always be the <u>first</u> to get paid the largest sum of upfront cash! This puts <u>you</u> in the driver's seat from day one!

■ **MILLIONAIRE SECRET #31**

The Wealth Making Secret That's So Simple That A 12-Year Old Child Could <u>Instantly</u> Discover The Perfect Way To Make A Giant Fortune In No Time Flat!

When you discover an opportunity that eliminates all of the headaches and hassles most people have to go through – you <u>will</u> have the perfect way to make money! And that is the true purpose of this letter. Our $100,000.00 A MONTH SYSTEM is a rare opportunity because it eliminates all of the mistakes that we see in almost every money-making opportunity that we investigate!

This is a wealth making secret that's so simple that a 12-year old child could <u>instantly</u> discover the perfect way to make a giant fortune in no time flat!

Now, that's a bold statement! But let me back it up with solid fact:

Our $100,000.00 A MONTH SYSTEM gives you the ultimate way to stay home and make money <u>without</u> all of the many headaches and hassles that most people are forced to go through!

Listen closely. **You can never know how great something is until you have something to compare it with.** And that's the real power behind the information in this book!

Now that you have some knowledge of all of the headaches and hassles that most people are going through – you are prepared to see just how great our $100,000.00 A MONTH SYSTEM really is!

So don't think I have been negative about all of this. I love business and I love entrepreneurs like you... And that's why I can't wait to slowly reveal all of the amazing details behind our $100,000.00 A MONTH SYSTEM! Go on to the next millionaire secret and I'll give you the seven reasons why this has the awesome power to make you super rich!

■ People ask the difference between a leader and a boss... The leader works in the open and the boss in covert. The leader leads and the boss drives.

Theodore Roosevelt

■ A leader is a dealer in hope.

Napoleon Bonaparte

■ We must not, in trying to think about how we can make a big difference, ignore the small daily differences we can make which, over time, add up to big differences that we often cannot foresee.

Marian Wright Edelman

■ MILLIONAIRE SECRET #32

The '7 Steps To Mega Wealth!' And Why They Can Make You Rich Beyond Your Wildest Dreams!

Our '$100,000 A MONTH SYSTEM!' discovery really is the perfect way to make money that you have been searching for <u>all</u> of your life! It meets ALL SEVEN of the requirements that we have established for the perfect business!

Here are those 7 requirements...

The perfect way to make money must have all of these major advantages:

1. You must be able to do everything from the comfort and privacy of your own home.

2. There must be many average people who are already making huge sums of money – and you must use their greatest secrets.

3. There must be a huge demand for the products and services being offered.

4. The items being offered <u>must</u> be high-ticket products or services that pay you HUGE margins of profit!

5. You must have the help, support, and guidance of people who truly understand how to make a fortune.

6. You must be able to make huge sums of money part-time! The amount of money you make must have nothing to do with the number of hours or the direct effort you put into it.

7. You must be able to make large sums of money <u>very quickly</u> – while also creating a predictable sum of monthly residual income that keeps growing bigger!

These are the '7 Steps To Mega Wealth!' And as you've seen, when you are involved in a business opportunity that has ALL SEVEN of these ingredients, you can become rich beyond your wildest dreams! These 7 items give you the perfect way to make money! And now you have <u>all seven</u> of them! Our '$100,000.00 A MONTH SYSTEM!' is the ultimate combination of all seven of these strong requirements for the perfect way to make money!

How To Turn A Few Thousand Dollars Into Millions Of Dollars In A Few Short Years!

Most business opportunities are simply too expensive for the average person. **This is a major problem because it forces people like you and me to <u>narrow</u> <u>our</u> <u>choices</u>.** Most people cannot afford to spend one million dollars to buy a McDonald's restaurant or invest in high-dollar commercial real estate or buy large blocks of stock in some high-tech company that is growing by leaps and bounds.

Listen. As you know by now, I am a full-time business opportunity investigator.

But there's one thing I didn't mention...

Here it is... Most of my Clients are <u>not</u> multi-millionaires who have hundreds of thousands of dollars to invest. So I spend 95% of my time researching low-cost business opportunities...

My mission is to discover unique opportunities that can be started for well under $10,000.00 and have the powerful potential to bring in millions every year!

Does that sound unbelievable? It's not.

Does this make you skeptical? It shouldn't.

You see, there are many people who started with less than $10,000.00 and ended up making many millions of dollars and, in some rare cases, billions of dollars for their owners! Yes, billions!

Making billions of dollars starting with almost nothing is truly rare – but there are many well-known examples of average people like you and me who have done it!

My 3 best examples come from the field of personal computers...

- **Michael Dell** started his company "Dell Computers" from his college dorm! His business grew so fast that he had to quit school! Now he's a multi-billionaire!

- **Steve Jobs and his partner, Steve Wozniak,** started "Apple Computer" from Steve's garage – <u>and</u> <u>he</u> was living at home with his mom and dad!

And my best story:

- **Bill Gates and his partner, Paul Allen,** started the multi-billion dollar money machine called "Microsoft" with less than $10,000.00! Bill was forced to drop out of school because business was booming and he knew if he didn't do something dramatic, he would lose a fortune. His father begged him to stay in school and told him he was ruining his life... But we all know how that story turned out!

Sure, these are isolated examples. But these examples have inspired me greatly! I have spent many years studying wealthy people to try to learn their secrets. And there is one thing I must tell you about:

Success Leaves Clues!

Please write this quote down and hang it on your wall or refrigerator or mirror.

Here's what it means:

If you want to get very rich – please "model" ordinary people who are already rich. In other words, find a group of average people who have and are getting rich. Discover <u>all</u> of their greatest secrets... Then try very hard to duplicate their exact actions! That's it! You must search for normal people who are making a huge fortune! This is how I developed our powerful new $100,000.00 A MONTH SYSTEM! This gives you the amazing secret that you can use to potentially turn a few thousand dollars into millions of dollars a few short years!

Remember, right now there are average people who are getting paid many thousands of dollars a month with this exciting opportunity!

And these people are <u>all</u> committing 3 deadly marketing mistakes! As you will see, this amazing opportunity eliminates each mistake and gives you all of the main benefits you would expect to receive if you invested huge sums of money in an expensive franchise!

■ MILLIONAIRE SECRET #34

Why many people are too smart to ever get rich.

Many of the smartest people I know are <u>afraid</u> to go into business for themselves. <u>Why?</u> The reason is simple: They know everything that can go wrong! They know how risky business can be. They already know about many of the problems we have gone over in this program.

They simply don't want to go through any of the headaches and hassles that we have talked about. And I don't blame them one bit! But these people are using their great brains the wrong way...

Yes, I see many people who are too smart to get rich! I hope you are <u>not</u> one of them! The major mistake all of these people make is this: They are using their great brain power the wrong way.

It sounds overly simplistic – but it's true!

I meet so many really smart people who will <u>never</u> get rich because they are <u>always</u> looking for what's <u>wrong</u> with every situation they face – instead of looking for what's right! This is the #1 reason why many people are too smart to ever get rich. But you don't have to let this happen to you! Remember, our '$100,000 A MONTH SYSTEM!' eliminates all of the problems that you are forced to go through with other business opportunities... This gives you and instant and almost unfair advantage over all of the other people who are in business today.

The Power Of "<u>Synergy</u>" And How It Can Make You More Money Than You Have Ever Dreamed Possible!

Most opportunities do not let you make money fast enough.

Here's the way it usually goes...

With most opportunities, you get very excited in the beginning – and you work very hard... You put in long hours, <u>but the money never comes in fast enough</u>. There's never enough money left over to pay all of the bills. Your whole life becomes a financial struggle. The bills keep coming in and there's never enough to pay them all... After awhile, the financial pressures wear you down. It's a losing battle until you finally throw in the towel! Your dream of having a successful business and becoming financially free is dead forever.

This is the story for millions of people. They are forced to go out of businesses each year because there is simply <u>not</u> enough money.

BUT THIS SHOULD <u>NEVER</u> HAPPEN TO YOU!

Listen closely, most opportunities are <u>not</u> set up to make you the kind of money you need to make because:

■ They are not built to pay you fast cash.

■ They're not built to pay you large amounts of money.

■ The markets for these businesses are too small.

■ There is very little demand for the items being offered.

■ The average dollar amount of each order is way too small.

There are other problems, too. But <u>those</u> are the main ones.

And these problems have been completely eliminated with our

$100,000.00 A MONTH SYSTEM!

Here's how our $100,000.00 A MONTH SYSTEM is designed to make you massive sums of cash that keeps coming to you for many years:

- The market for the items you'll be offering is huge! This marketplace is made up of tens of millions of people who are easy to reach and badly want the items we offer!

- The demand for the items we offer is big now – and only getting bigger! As you'll see, the best years for all of the items in this System are still ahead! In fact, <u>the future is so bright you gotta wear shades</u>!

- Our marketing system is designed to pay you huge sums of money very quickly! Everything is designed to let you deposit the largest amount of cash in the fastest time – with the least effort!

We can do everything for you... This gets you off to a super fast and profitable start! You'll have the awesome power of momentum working for you from day one! This is the ultimate way to tap into the power of "<u>synergy</u>" – and potentially make more money than you have ever dreamed possible!

- General Dwight D. Eisenhower used a simple device to illustrate the art of leadership. Laying an ordinary piece of string on a table, he'd illustrate how you could easily pull it in any direction. "Try and push it, though," he cautioned, "and it won't go anywhere. It's just that way when it comes to leading people."

- Never look down to test the ground before taking your next step; only he who keeps his eye fixed on the far horizon will find the right road.

Dag Hammarskjold

GUARANTEED WEALTH!
Here Is The <u>One</u> <u>Secret</u> That Opens Up The Floodgates And Lets The Money Pour In!

The same secrets that are making huge sums of money for one person can make huge sums for you, too! You must discover everything that they are doing right and everything that they are doing wrong! Just do more of the things that they're doing right and eliminate all of the things that they're doing wrong! This is the amazing secret that can give you GUARANTEED WEALTH! It is the <u>one</u> <u>secret</u> that can open up the floodgates and lets the money pour in!

Yes, getting rich can be this simple!

This isn't rocket science!

All you are doing is repeating the actions that others are already using to get paid giant sums of money!

Listen closely. People do not get rich by accident. There's <u>always</u> a reason why people become wealthy. Most of the time it comes down to a few very simple things:

- They have stumbled onto the right opportunity – at the right time. Timing is everything!

- The items they offer to their market are unique and badly wanted by the people who buy them.

- There are huge profit margins built into all of these products.

- They had the right help – every step of the way.

- They are part of a growing trend.

That's it! There are probably a few other possibilities – but these are the main areas that make average people very rich!

And now you have all of these amazing benefits working for you...to help you make huge sums of money with our $100,000.00 A MONTH SYSTEM!

This unique opportunity combines 3 multi-billion dollar emerging markets. All of these markets are BIG now – and only getting bigger! The best years are still ahead! Many more people will be getting rich in all three of these emerging markets and you can be one of them!

The products and services being offered are totally unique! They are in-demand, high-ticket items that have a great deal of high-perceived value and a huge profit margin. This lets you stay home and get paid huge sums of money for very few transactions that are made for you by our marketing system! The system does all of the selling!

■ MILLIONAIRE SECRET #37

How Our System Is Designed To Make You Tens Of Thousands Of Dollars A Month While You Shop, Sleep, Or Are On Vacation!

Our '$100,000 A MONTH SYSTEM!' gives you so many advantages that the other people who are already getting rich do not have:

- You'll reach people they're not reaching.

- You will never have to do any personal selling!

- You will be in the powerful position to make huge sums of money – regardless of the number of hours you put in!

This gives you the advantages of the rich:

- The amount of money you can make is not dependent on the number of hours you put in.

- Your marketing system can make you money while you are

shopping, sleeping, or on vacation!

- You can spend more time doing the things you love the most and still make huge sums of money.

Add it up. You'll see. These are the amazing ways that our system is designed to make you tens of thousands of dollars a month while you shop, sleep, or are on vacation!

This lets you do everything part-time — from the comfort, privacy, and security of your own home.

Working from home is a great joy! You spend a lot of time with your family. You have the satisfaction of knowing that you are doing something that few others can do.

But many opportunities cannot be done from home. You must meet with clients, prospects, staff, and suppliers on a daily basis. Your whole life is wrapped up in one meeting after another. You never have the time to do the things you love to do.

Many ambitious people end up making all of the money they dreamed of making — but they lose their family in the process.

- They work very long hours away from home.

- They're <u>always</u> on the road — flying here and there.

- The constant travel burns them out and drives a major wedge between them and their spouses.

But these people have no choice! They chose a business opportunity that forces them to be "out in the field" on a daily basis. You cannot afford to do this...

Listen closely. When I am researching a new opportunity I <u>always</u> ask myself one question, *"Can it be done from home?"* If the answer is *"No!"* then I move on! It's not the perfect way to make money if your whole life must be spent away from the people you love.

Getting Rich From Home Is As Simple As Saying "<u>YES!</u>" To These 3 Questions!

The secret to getting rich from home and <u>only</u> putting in the hours you want to put in is rather simple: Just find an opportunity that has been designed and built to let you do this.

It sounds so simple, doesn't it?

But it's true!

In fact, getting rich from home is as simple as saying "<u>YES!</u>" to these 3 simple questions:

1. Can you make sales <u>without</u> your personal involvement? Is there a marketing system in place that does all of this for you?

2. Can all of the fulfillment of the products or services be done for you?

3. Can the customer service work be done for you?

That's it!

As you can see, these are 3 very easy questions... But don't think they're too easy... They're not. *In fact*...

If the answer to all three of these questions is *"YES!"* then you have the perfect way to make money!

All of the sales are made for you by your marketing system. Plus, all of the fulfillment of the products and services is handled for you! *And to top it off:* all of the customer service work is done for you!

There is nothing left for you to do <u>except</u> deposit the checks into your bank account!

And now you have all three of these things working for you!

The 10 Ways We Can Help You Make <u>GIANT</u> <u>SUMS</u> Of Money Right Now!

Our $100,000.00 A MONTH SYSTEM lets you make money without having to spend all of your time doing all of the things that 99% of all other businesspeople are <u>forced</u> to do! Everything is done for you!

This lets you stay home and make huge sums of money <u>without</u> any of the headaches and hassles that most people are forced to go through.

You'll have 10 powerful ways to make <u>GIANT</u> <u>SUMS</u> of money right now, without any of the headaches and hassles that most other business people are forced to go through!

Here they are:

1. NO employees
2. NO storefront
3. NO daily commute
4. NO long hours
5. NO overhead expenses
6. NO meetings!
7. NO personal selling
8. NO shipping of products
9. NO contact with others <u>unless</u> you want it!
10. NONE of the headaches that most people are forced to go through!

Does all of this sound too good to be true?

Well, it is for the average person!

But it's <u>not</u> for you!

All you did was choose a home-based business that was not dependent upon...

> ■ In his later years, Winston Churchill was asked to give the commencement address at Oxford University. Following his introduction, he rose, went to the podium, and said, "Never, never, never give up." Then he took his seat.

- **A local market**
- **Personal selling**
- **Fulfillment and customer service**

Please listen carefully... Most people go into business for themselves in the most unconscious way. They <u>never</u> think it through. They put very little thought in to choosing the <u>right</u> opportunity that is perfectly suited for the life they want to live.

<u>YOU CANNOT MAKE THIS MISTAKE</u>. The business you choose <u>must</u> be custom built around the perfect life you want to live.

You must build your business around your ideal lifestyle. You don't want to build your life around your business.

Your business must serve <u>you</u> rather than you serving it. Most people will <u>never</u> figure this out. They choose the wrong business and now their whole life is a living nightmare.

Now they are working way too many hours for too little pay.

Now they are forced to do many things for money that they <u>hate</u> doing. This makes me so sad.

And you will NEVER worry about making this mistake!

Our $100,000.00 A MONTH SYSTEM is <u>not</u> dependent on the number of hours you work – or the activities you are <u>directly</u> involved with on a daily basis. These opportunities <u>are</u> <u>rare</u> – but they do exist! In fact, you have one here!

A Billionaire's Secret That Can Make You An Instant Millionaire Right Now!

The markets for your products and services must be <u>HUGE</u> and growing quickly! There must be a genuine demand for the items you offer.

Large growing markets create many <u>new</u> opportunities that can make you very wealthy.

Billionaire, Ted Turner, once said, *"It's all about demand and supply!"* He was right! **You don't have to be a genius to figure this out! As long as the demand for whatever you are offering exceeds the supply – you'll be able to get very rich!** <u>Just make sure you pick the right area in the first place.</u> *Here's how...*

■ Find markets that are growing quickly.

■ Find markets where many people are already getting rich.

■ Look for markets that are changing fast!

This is a billionaire's secret that can make you an instant millionaire right now! The secret is to find markets that are changing rapidly...

Why fast changing markets?

That's easy...

Fast changing markets are where the <u>biggest</u> opportunities for getting super rich are! These markets create all kinds of exciting new ways to get rich!

With these markets, there's all kinds of room for many different people to make HUGE sums of money!

And this is great news for you!

Why? Because...

Our $100,000.00 A MONTH SYSTEM is comprised of 3 multi-billion dollar markets that are growing by leaps and bounds! These markets are all part of explosive future trends that will create many new millionaires and even billionaires!

Listen closely. Most people <u>never</u> get rich because they choose the wrong areas to get into.

- They choose items with little demand.

- They choose small markets.

- They choose markets that are tired and worn out.

These people are frustrated because they're always struggling for every dollar that they make. But what they don't know is that they chose the wrong market to begin with...

One of the richest people I personally know has this to say:

"When you ride a billion-dollar wave – you create many new millionaires... <u>automatically!</u>"

This is true! Emerging markets make people super rich! All you have to do is look for the hottest areas with the biggest growth!

Many average people are multi-millionaires – and even billionaires – because they simply choose the right market to get into. They caught THE BILLION-DOLLAR WAVE and then rode it in for major wealth! And now you can do this, too!

Our $100,000.00 A MONTH SYSTEM is a powerful combination of 3 of the most explosive markets that are already putting GIANT sums of money in many people's personal bank accounts!

Here is the formula for major wealth! I call this formula "The 5 Keys To Wealth" –

1. **There must be an established demand for the items you sell.** Look for the hottest areas that are creating the largest number of brand new millionaires!

2. **What you offer to satisfy the hunger of this market must be totally unique!** There must be something powerful that separates it from everything else!

3. **It must address the tremendous skepticism in the market.** If it's too new, people will be afraid. And scared people do <u>not</u> buy... You <u>must</u> have a solid answer for all of these very skeptical people.

4. **It must have built in residual income.** There must be something within the opportunity that lets you build this residual income that continues to come to you automatically.

5. **There must also be a high-ticket item or items within your mix of products and services.** This will help you cover <u>all</u> of your overhead expenses and pay yourself a nice income!

Here's the good news:

**Our $100,000.00 A Month System has
all five of these golden keys!**

The more you know about our $100,000.00 A MONTH SYSTEM, the more you will realize how this gives you ALL of the key ingredients you need to get rich. But for now, let's look at the next powerful ingredient you need to make the largest sum of money in the minimum amount of time...

The items being offered must be high-ticket products and services that pay you the largest sum of money for the smallest number of transactions.

Most business people go broke because there are simply not enough sales and profits to cover all of their ever-growing expenses.

This sounds like common sense, right?

**Well, it is! And yet as the great American philosopher,
Mark Twain, once said: *"Common sense is a very
uncommon thing!"***

***Mark said this in the 1800's...* <u>But</u> <u>it's</u> <u>even</u> <u>more</u> <u>true</u>
<u>today</u>!**

Remember, most people choose opportunities in a very
unconscious way. They go into businesses they think will be fun and
interesting. They never ask themselves, *"Can this make me rich?"*
Or, *"How will I make the largest amount of money with this?"*

Their decision to go into the business is purely emotional.
They never stop and think it through. But you <u>cannot</u> afford to do
this! Sure, you need to choose a business that is fun and rewarding.

You need a business that you can fall in love with...

But your business <u>must</u> also be able to make you GIANT sums
of money! You need to offer products and services that people
really want... These must be items that sell for premium sums of
money.

**As long as you choose the right market where the
demand exceeds the supply, and you sell items that fill that
demand in a whole new and exciting way, then you will be in
the powerful position to sell these high-ticket items for the
most money!**

You should <u>never</u> be afraid to offer products and services for
premium prices – **as long as the value of what you offer is
greater than the amount you charge – it's okay to charge
premium prices!** As long as the demand is there and what you
offer is unique – then people are <u>more</u> than willing to give you
huge sums of their money in exchange for whatever you're offering.

And that's the beauty of our $100,000.00 A MONTH SYSTEM!

<u>HERE'S</u> <u>HOW</u> <u>THIS</u> <u>IS</u> <u>DESIGNED</u> <u>TO</u> <u>MAKE</u> <u>YOU</u> <u>RICH</u>: You

will sit back and let our proven marketing system offer items that have a great deal of perceived value to the people who badly want and need them... However, because these items are fulfilled via the modern miracle of the Internet, the actual cost to distribute them is amazingly low!

These are the main wealth-building secrets behind our $100,000.00 A MONTH SYSTEM:

SECRET #1:

The value of the items you will offer is very high! And the demand is also very high! In fact, people are spending billions of dollars right now to receive the benefits of these items!

SECRET #2:

And yet, thanks to the modern miracle of technology, the actual cost to deliver these items is dirt-cheap.

This is the simple secret behind this amazing opportunity that could potentially be worth hundreds of thousands – or even millions of dollars – to you!

■ **MILLIONAIRE SECRET #41**

How To Separate The Few Real Opportunities From All Of The Fakes And Frauds.

You must have the help, support, and guidance of people who truly understand how to turn small sums of money into a huge fortune! These people must earn the bulk of their money by doing everything they can to help you get rich!

Many people claim that they want to help you get rich, but do they really? There's only one way you can know for sure...

Just ask yourself these questions:

■ **How much money are they making?** Unless someone

has already made a huge sum of money for themselves — chances are they can't help you.

- **Do they earn the bulk of their profits by helping you make money?** If the answer is *"NO"* then <u>where</u> is their incentive to do everything they can to help you get rich?

- **Is their opportunity already making huge sums of money for other people?** Again, if the answer is *"NO"* you <u>cannot</u> afford to waste your precious time and money on their untested plans and programs.

- If you would hit the mark, you must aim a little above it; every arrow that flies feels the attraction of earth.

    Henry Wadsworth Longfellow

- Not failure, but low aim, is crime.

    James Russell Lowell

- The harder you work, the luckier you get.

    Gary Player

These questions let you quickly and easily separate the <u>few real opportunities</u> from all of the fakes and frauds. These three main questions sound like common sense — but you would be <u>shocked</u> to know that **most people <u>never</u> ask these questions!**

These people get caught up in the emotion of the opportunity. They want to get rich so badly — they <u>never</u> ask themselves the three questions above that could make all the difference.

What's worse — if they <u>did</u> ask themselves these questions — the answer would be a big fat *"NO!"* to each one. It's true. If you ask most home based business opportunity promoters these 3 questions <u>and, if they were honest with you</u>, the answer to each question would be *"NO!"*

That brings us to the 3 biggest problems most people face when looking for a way to stay home and make money:

Problem #1 — Many people who sell get-rich-quick materials are <u>not</u> rich themselves! This may seem ironic — but it's true! How can someone who has <u>never</u> made any significant sum of money help you get rich? They can't. And you know it. This is like the blind leading the blind.

And that leads us <u>directly</u> to the next problem...

Problem #2 — **Most promoters make the bulk of their profits on the opportunities they sell.** They have <u>no</u> great incentive to help you succeed. They sell you their programs and leave you out in the cold.

And last, but not least...

Problem #3 — **Many of the opportunities being sold today have not been proven to make any significant money for *anyone* but the promoters themselves.** I am <u>shocked</u> and amazed at how many unproven plans and programs are being sold to unsuspecting people like you and me. This makes me very sad and angry.

But again, here is where our $100,000.00 A MONTH SYSTEM stands head and shoulders above <u>every</u> <u>other</u> <u>opportunity</u> that we have investigated! The answer to each one of the 3 questions I just gave you is *"<u>YES!</u>"* – *"<u>YES!</u>"* – *"<u>YES!</u>"*

Question #1 — **Do the people behind this opportunity have a strong track record for helping folks get rich?**

"YES!" We have used the same powerful methods that have gone into our $100,000.00 A MONTH SYSTEM to make millions of dollars! **They've made us millions and that's why we firmly believe that they have the power to make you millions, too!**

Question #2 — **Do we earn the bulk of our profits by doing everything to help you succeed?**

"**YES!**" With our $100,000.00 A MONTH SYSTEM – we have the ultimate incentive to do <u>all</u> that we can to help you make the largest sum of money in the fastest period of time! **The bulk of our profits come from helping you get off to an extremely successful and profitable start!** The more we can do to help you – the more money we will make!

Question #3 – Is the opportunity already making average people huge sums of money?

"**YES!**" As you know, the reason we call this the $100,000.00 A MONTH SYSTEM is because people are already making $50,000.00 to $100,000.00 a month right now! And our System completely eliminates some of the major mistakes that all of them are making!

■ **MILLIONAIRE SECRET #42**

ABSOLUTE PROOF That You Really Can Get Rich With This Amazing Discovery!

You must have a marketing system that does all of the selling for you.

You must have a powerful marketing system that makes money for you... automatically! This system must be built from the ground up to sell to the growing number of skeptical people...

As you know, many average people are already making tens of thousands of dollars a month with the basic discovery behind our $100,000.00 A MONTH SYSTEM. **This is all of the proof that you need that this is a System that can truly make you rich!** Remember, if one average person with no special knowledge or experience is getting rich – then <u>you</u> can get rich, too!

This isn't rocket science...

All you have to do is find average people who have no special abilities, who are getting very rich, and then duplicate their exact steps. That's what you'll be doing when you use this new $100,000.00 A MONTH SYSTEM!

The fact that others were already getting rich with this opportunity was the #1 thing that excited me in the beginning! It should excite you, too!

But there's ONE MAJOR PROBLEM on your path to riches...

It's the simple fact that most of the people who are already making giant sums of money with this opportunity are also doing a great deal of personal selling.

This is terrible for one main reason:

If you're like me – you hate to sell.

If you're like me – you don't want to deal with all of the problems of personal selling:

- You hate getting hung up on.

- You hate getting doors slammed in your face.

- You hate bugging people by trying to sell them the things they don't want.

Listen closely. I used to sell for a living and I've been hung up on and had many doors slammed in my face! But I had to do this to stay in my first business I started in December of 1985. So I did this for a few years and it was miserable!

Then, a few years later, my wife and I discovered Direct Response Marketing! And when we did – our entire lives were changed forever!

Direct Response Marketing is a powerful method of reaching and selling to thousands – or even millions – of people without any rejection. Yes, it's true! All of the selling is done for you by the special Direct Response materials and the system of getting those materials into the right hands. When you do this successfully – you can quickly make millions of dollars!

This is ABSOLUTE PROOF that you really can get rich with this amazing discovery!

Does this sound too good to be true? It's not!

Direct Response Marketing generates 275 billion dollars a year!

This powerful method of selling has made many average people like my wife, Eileen, and I multi-millionaires! It can make <u>you</u> rich, too!

Best of all, the greatest Direct Response Marketing secrets that have made us tens of millions of dollars have been built into our $100,000.00 A MONTH SYSTEM!

This lets you cash in with the same basic opportunity that others are already using to make up to $100,000.00 a month without any of the hassles that they are <u>forced</u> to go through:

- You'll never speak to anyone!

- You'll <u>never</u> have any personal rejection!

- You'll never have to convince anyone of anything!

Our proven System does all of this, and more, for you!

As you have seen, our $100,000.00 A MONTH SYSTEM gives you the main ingredients that you need to make huge sums of money from the comfort of your own home! Remember, if you have everything we've covered so far in this book working for you – you can get very rich!

■ MILLIONAIRE SECRET #43

The Single Most Important Thing You Can Do To Get Huge Sums Of Money For Life!

There must be an established and growing market for the business you are getting into.

The market you decide to get into is the single most important thing that you can do to achieve enormous success. Pick this market right and you have the power to make all of the money that you have ever wanted... Choose the wrong market and you can face many years of problems, headaches, and hassles...

Many people <u>never</u> get rich because they choose the wrong market. They are <u>way</u> too focused on the product or service they want to sell instead of the people they want to sell to.

Not making this mistake and putting all of your focus on 'the market' of people you are trying to sell to is the single most important thing that you can do to get huge sums of money for life!

Here are the ingredients for the perfect market that can make you rich: >> It must be established. >> There must be many average people who are already getting rich! >> It must be easy to reach. >> And it must be HUGE – but *still* growing quickly...

The biggest opportunities to get rich quick are in fast growing markets. These markets are changing quickly. The demand for all kinds of products and services in these markets is strong. This sets the stage for many people like you and me to make millions!

■ **MILLIONAIRE SECRET #44**

The Time-Tested 4-Step Formula For Getting Rich In The Fastest Time, With The Least Amount Of Effort!

Many people never get rich because: *1.* The market for their products or services is too small. *2.* There is little demand for what they offer. *3.* The markets are too established and the products and services they sell have been reduced to commodities. *4.* Or, in some cases, they are ahead of the timing curve and there is <u>no</u> real market for whatever they sell.

When people ask me: ***"What is your best advice for those of us who want to get rich in the fastest time, with the least*** *amount of effort?"*

I always give them this simple formula:

- Find average people who are <u>already</u> getting rich.

- Discover what these people are doing to earn all of their wealth.

- Find out what they are doing right and wrong. Become one of their customers or find some creative way to spy on them!

- Then duplicate their actions! Try to do <u>more</u> of what you see them doing right <u>and</u> <u>correct</u> the mistakes they're making.

That's it! This is as simple as it can be to get very rich! This is the time-tested 4-step formula for getting rich in the fastest time, with the least amount of effort!

■ An obstacle is something you see when you take your eyes off the goal.

■ Never look back unless you are planning to go that way.

■ A great man shows his greatness by the way he treats little men.

    Thomas Carlyle

■ There's always room at the top.

■ Most people would succeed in small things if they were not troubled with great ambitions.

    Henry Wadsworth Longfellow

■ Courage is grace under pressure.

    Ernest Hemingway

Remember this: the pioneers got scalped!

You must go into areas that are making other average people rich right now! Look for people with no special skills or abilities who are making millions. **Remember – the same activities that are making one person super rich can make you rich, too!** Later – when you have millions of dollars in the bank and you want to flex your muscles – you can try bold new things... But in the beginning you must follow the people who are *already* getting super rich... And that brings us to the next millionaire secret. Read on...

■ **MILLIONAIRE SECRET #45**

A Simple Way To Get Huge Sums Of Money Flowing To You Right Away!

Remember, getting rich is simple: just find out what other very successful people are doing to make all of their money... Then duplicate their actions and correct as many of the mistakes they're making as you can. That's it! Just do this and the money will start flowing to you. This is the secret we used to discover our new $100,000.00 A MONTH SYSTEM! It's the simple way to get huge sums of money flowing to you right away!

Here's how we developed this amazing wealth system:

- We discovered many average people who were already making tens of thousands of dollars a month.

- We studied them.

- We found out what they were doing right and wrong.

- Then we created our $100,000.00 A MONTH SYSTEM that eliminated the mistakes they were making!

That's it!

Don't over think it: Getting rich very quickly can be this simple.

But there's a second key to getting rich that is just as important...

You must offer something new or different that sets you apart from all of the other competitors in the booming market you choose.

The products or services you pick are secondary to the market itself... However, you must choose the right items if you want the money to start flowing your way.

So what are the right items?

Simple.

The perfect products and services that can make you a millionaire in no time flat are <u>new</u> and exciting items that fill some type of serious problem in the marketplace.

And this is the secret behind our $100,000.00 A MONTH SYSTEM!

I'll give you all the amazing secrets about the products behind this opportunity... You'll be thrilled when you see how this has the power to make you very rich! But for now, you must realize how these two magic keys can make you very rich...

<u>**CONSIDER THIS**</u>:

Average people are getting rich with <u>BOTH</u> of these magic keys:

- They are offering their products or services in an established and growing market.

- They are offering this market something very unique that nobody else has!

Best of all, our new $100,000.00 A MONTH SYSTEM lets you tap into the power of BOTH of these magic keys to wealth!

The <u>ONE</u> <u>SIMPLE</u> <u>QUESTION</u> that can get huge sums of money <u>RUSHING</u> <u>IN</u> so fast that you won't believe it's really happening!

ASK YOURSELF THIS QUESTION: What can you say or do that will eliminate their fears and make them want to give their money to you? Answer this question in the greatest way – and the money can come RUSHING IN so fast, you won't believe it's really happening!

Listen closely. Skepticism is a growing problem.

We are living in a period of time where more and more people are skeptical than ever before in history...

This is a growing problem <u>that</u> 99% of the people in business never face head-on...

You cannot afford to make this mistake.

You must wake up to the fact that the people you want to reach and do business with are skeptical and probably do not believe a word you're saying... These people have been lied to, misled, and cheated too many times. Now they don't trust anyone... They're <u>always</u> asking themselves, *"What's the catch? What isn't he or she telling me?"*

If you don't have a solid reason or reasons <u>why</u> you are offering them such a great opportunity – you will lose them forever!

This is what is happening right now with all of the people who are already making many tens of thousands of dollars a month with the basic secrets that make up the foundation of our $100,000.00 A MONTH SYSTEM. In fact, this is <u>one</u> of the 3 deadly mistakes that <u>all</u> of these people are making in spite of their success. These people are making some really terrible mistakes and scaring off <u>all</u> of

the very best prospects!

They have <u>no</u> answers for all of the skeptical people... They are like so many other people we see who are burying their heads in the sand, and it's costing them huge sums of money that can now be going straight to you!

The reason why is simple...

Our $100,000.00 A MONTH SYSTEM eliminates this major mistake!

Our system was built for skeptical people! We are <u>not</u> burying our heads in the sand! We have <u>a</u> <u>very</u> <u>solid</u> <u>answer</u> for all of the skeptical people. This is just <u>one</u> of the major advantages we have over all of the other people who are <u>already</u> making tens of thousands of dollars a month. But it's a powerful one that can make you rich!

■ **MILLIONAIRE SECRET #47**

How to get a steady ongoing stream of residual income that grows BIGGER and <u>never</u> stops coming to you!

As you know, there are thousands of different kinds of businesses out there that offer a never-ending assortment of products and services. On the surface these businesses all look different. **But the one thing all businesses have in common is the fact that they <u>must</u> serve their customers and make a profit.**

But making steady profits year after year is hard to do...

The costs to run a business can be very high. The markets fluctuate due to seasons or the economy... In other words, some months and years are generally <u>better</u> than others. **The amount of money that comes to you rises and falls. But the bills you must pay to stay in business keep coming no matter what!** <u>These</u> <u>bills</u> <u>must</u> <u>be</u> <u>paid,</u> <u>regardless</u> <u>of</u> <u>the</u> <u>amount</u> <u>of</u> <u>money</u> that's

<u>coming in</u>.

Listen closely. Many millions of businesses are forced to close their doors each year. They simply can't get enough money to keep the doors open. They go bankrupt or just quit. Tens of millions of people suffer because of these companies who go out of business.

But no company ever went out of business because they were making too many sales and profits!

Think about this! People go out of business because they have too little money – not because they have too much money!

THE BOTTOM LINE:

Having residual income that comes to you automatically on a regular basis is your greatest insurance policy that you will <u>always</u> have plenty of money – <u>no</u> matter what happens to your business. This gives you the freedom and power that most people can <u>only</u> dream of!

Millions of businesses fail each year because they simply don't have enough 'residual income' that comes to them automatically... By finding an opportunity that provides this type of income to you, you'll make sure it <u>never</u> happens to you!

So how do you get this automatic residual income?

Well, that's different for every business.

But here is the simplest general way to do it: You must offer products or services that have ongoing fees of some kind attached to them. These additional services will continue to come to your customers on a regular basis – <u>until</u> they tell you to STOP!

You make one simple transaction one time and then keep delivering the best value possible and the money can keep growing bigger and bigger and never stop coming to you! Again, these ongoing fees are different for each business and market. But this is the basic secret behind getting paid an ongoing income that <u>never</u> stops. Best of all, our '$100,000 A MONTH SYSTEM!' is a unique 'non-MLM' opportunity that is designed to pay you huge sums of automatic residual income! This can give you a steady ongoing stream of residual income that grows BIGGER and <u>never</u> stops!

■ Fear always springs from ignorance.

Ralph Waldo Emerson

■ Courage is very important. Like a muscle, it is strengthened by use.

Ruth Gordon

■ Don't be afraid to take a big step if one is indicated. You can't cross a chasm in two small jumps.

David Lloyd George

■ Be willing to make decisions. That's the most important quality in a good leader. Don't fall victim to what I call the "ready-aim-aim-aim-aim syndrome." You must be willing to fire.

T. Boone Pickens

■ **MILLIONAIRE SECRET #48**

Why Millions Of Businesses Fail Each Year... And How To Make Sure It <u>Never</u> Happens To You!

You must have at least one item in your mix of products and services that pays HUGE profits!

The sale of this high-ticket item will help you cover your overhead expenses and give you a nice paycheck!

The problem: Most businesspeople are simply working too many hours for too little pay.

There's <u>never</u> enough money left over for them <u>after</u> all of the bills are paid. They are <u>always</u> struggling for every dollar that comes in – and there's <u>never</u> enough of them... This is the reason why millions of businesses fail each year...

It's a constant headache and hassle.

They're always worried about money. And they get sick and tired of the constant strain and struggle. Finally, they can no longer take it and they quit.

Listen. Millions of businesses go bankrupt every year because there simply is not enough money to cover all of their growing costs.

And the solution is so simple...

<u>Just</u> <u>make</u> <u>more</u> <u>money</u>!

It sounds simple – and it really is!

All you need is at least one product or service that I call "The Slack Adjuster!" This is at least one high-ticket item that pays you huge profits.

Most businesses do not have this and their entire life is one major financial struggle after another. Their struggle never ends. There's simply never enough money left over to pay themselves and build their nest egg.

So if this seems like common sense – it's not!

The fact is: This is a very simple idea that most businesspeople have <u>never</u> thought of! And even the ones who have considered it <u>still</u> don't know how to implement it. They have no idea of how to find or develop a high-ticket, high-profit margin product or service. But now you will never make this mistake... Our '$100,000 A MONTH SYSTEM!' lets you cash in from the sales (that we can make for you!) of high-ticket, high-profit products that can put huge sums of money into your bank account!

The #1 REASON Why Most Opportunities Will <u>Never</u> Make You Rich... And Why Ours Will!

Many businesses are built around selling low-ticket items for paper thin profit margins. The markets are small or highly competitive. The products and services have been reduced to commodities. This is the #1 reason most opportunities will never make you rich.

But here is the golden secret...

If you do a great job of picking the right market and separating yourself from the other companies in your market – you will have the power to easily get paid huge sums of money! Yes, this will put you in the strongest position to get rich.

Here's why:

- Fast-growing markets produce incredible demand!

- This demand is almost insatiable! And in some markets it is insatiable. It has no end... People can't get enough!

- The demand becomes so great that if you will simply choose the right items that are truly unique – then it will be so much easier to find or develop the <u>right</u> high-ticket products and services that let you pay <u>all</u> of your bills with plenty of money left over for you!

And this is the amazing wealth secret behind our $100,000.00 A MONTH SYSTEM!

Everything is in place for you to get paid massive sums of money:

- The demand for all 3 of the emerging multi-billion markets is <u>so</u> strong – and the items we offer are so unique – it makes it <u>easy</u> to ask for and receive huge sums of money!

- People are happy to pay the high prices because of the tremendous value they receive in exchange for their money!

- The perceived value is super high. But thanks to the miracle of technology, the actual cost to deliver these items is low!

These ingredients give you a tremendous power that most businesspeople can only dream of... Their dream will be your reality!

■ **MILLIONAIRE SECRET #50**

Say "<u>YES!</u>" To These 12 Simple Questions And Be Set For Life!

Here is the <u>OLDEST WEALTH-MAKING FORMULA</u> that we have used at our company, Mid-American Opportunity Research Enterprises, Inc. (a.k.a. M.O.R.E., Incorporated) since we first began investigating business and money-making opportunities back in 1988. This formula worked for us in 1988 — and helped us to pick the <u>few</u> million-dollar winners from <u>all</u> of the losers. And it works just as well today! So please read carefully...

Since 1988 we have been searching for simple formulas that we can quickly use to identify the greatest wealth-making opportunities to separate them from all of the others.

As you know, when it comes to money-making plans and programs, all that glitters is not gold!

Most of the plans and programs on the market *"claim"* to be the very best. > There is <u>always</u> something to get us excited. > There is always some BIG promise about this opportunity. > Some new-fangled technology. > Some exciting new secret formula...

<u>YOU KNOW WHAT I'M TALKING ABOUT</u>.

All of the plans and programs promise that they are totally different than all of the others. They <u>all</u> *"claim"* to be <u>the one</u> <u>program</u> that will turn everything around for you! > The one that will make you a millionaire in no time flat! **>** The one program that will change your life forever! **>** The one that will create an endless river of cash to flow in to your life and <u>never</u> stop!

Do these plans and programs really exist?

YES, THEY DO!

But they are very hard to find.

In fact, searching for the perfect money-making program is like trying to find a needle in a haystack! It's almost impossible!

That's why you need the **<u>ACID TEST FORMULAS</u>** that we use to separate fact from fiction. Here's the oldest test, that we have been using since 1988, to separate the programs that can make you millions of dollars from all of the others.

Just get a 'YES!' answer to these 12 very simple questions and you can be set for life:

1. Are average people already making huge sums of money?

2. Can the opportunity be started for <u>less</u> money than most people can come up with for something they really want?

3. **Is it possible to get thousands of dollars coming in fast?**

4. Can everything be done from home?

5. Can someone make huge sums of money part-time?

6. **Is it possible to make millions of dollars?**

7. **Can it be done with ZERO personal selling?**

8. Is there help and guidance available from capable people who have a strong track record for making large sums of money?

9. Is this a long-term moneymaker?

10. Can it produce automatic residual income?

11. Is it easy to start?

12. Is there an <u>exit</u> strategy?

That's it! Just ask yourself these 12 very simple questions. If the answer to <u>only</u> <u>half</u> of them is "YES!" then you <u>know</u> you have stumbled onto a red-hot program that has the power to make you huge sums of money!

Is the answer is "YES!" to <u>all</u> 12 questions, then you can be on your way to getting very rich!

We have been putting each new opportunity through this very simple 12-question test since 1988.

It has helped us do the one major thing that you must do:

Avoid <u>all</u> of the opportunities that will <u>never</u> make you rich <u>no</u> <u>matter</u> <u>how</u> <u>hard</u> <u>you</u> <u>work</u> – from the few opportunities that have the potential power to make you a millionaire in <u>no</u> time flat!

- Please write these questions down and hang them on your wall.

- Then ask yourself these 12 very simple questions each and every time that you are faced with a new "once-in-a-lifetime" opportunity.

- **Do this and you'll be shocked to realize that with most opportunities you will hit a big fat "<u>NO</u>!" before you get to Question #4!!!**

Yes, this is the exciting thing about this simple 12-question acid test:

Most of the money-making opportunities we look at can't

> ■ Talk without effort is nothing.
>
> *Maria W. Stewart*
>
> ■ Always behave like a duck — keep calm and unruffled on the surface but paddle like the devil underneath.
>
> *Lord Barbizon*
>
> ■ If you are not part of the solution, you are part of the problem.
>
> *Eldridge Cleaver*

even make it past the first 3 questions!

Question #1 — Are average people getting rich with this opportunity right now? *"NO!"* The only people getting rich are the promoters themselves and the superstars at the top!

Question #2 — Can the opportunity be started for the amount of money most people can scrape together for something they really want? **Again, the answer is "NO WAY!"** Most business opportunities that get past the first question will almost always <u>fail</u> on this second question! Most business opportunities that are making average people rich are expensive franchises that cost many tens or even hundreds of thousands of dollars.

Listen. If you want a surefire way to become a millionaire, all you have to do is invest in a McDonald's or Kentucky Fried Chicken franchise. This is your <u>safest</u> bet. But who has the $500,000.00 to $1,000,000.00 cash it takes to get into one of these deals?

So, as you can see, even though there are 12 questions on our list, most opportunities will <u>never</u> get past the first two!

But some opportunities do get beyond these first two questions. In fact, there are many low-cost opportunities that the average person can start for very little money. <u>And a few of these opportunities are actually making some people very rich!</u>

We spend 90% of our time investigating these low-cost business opportunities. Most of them <u>never</u> get past the next five questions. In fact, the answer to the third question is almost always "NO!"

Here it is...

Question #3 – Is it possible to start making many thousands of dollars right away? **Again, the answer is a BIG FAT "NO!" for most of the low-cost business opportunities that we investigate.** It's true there are many exciting opportunities that the average person can start for little money. And some of these opportunities are even making some of these people very rich! But when we study the successes of these opportunities, we usually find that almost all of these super-successful people had to go through many years of pain and struggle before the money began flowing into their lives. In fact, most of the opportunities that can be started for very little money also produce very little money – <u>especially</u> in the beginning when you are first getting started.

However, as you are about to see, this amazing new wealth-maker passes this bulletproof test with flying colors! In fact, the answer to each one of these very difficult questions is **A BIG FAT "YES!"**

■ **MILLIONAIRE SECRET #51**

How Average People Are Making More Money Than Many Doctors Or Lawyers Make... Even Though They're Doing 3 Really Stupid Things!

You will be shocked and amazed when you see how much money other people are making with the basic wealth-making secret that we have discovered – in spite of some really terrible mistakes they're <u>all</u> making!

You'll be so excited when you discover how average people are making more money than many doctors and lawyers make, in spite of doing 3 really stupid things!

But that's not all...

With this amazing opportunity, you can get started for less than you'd spend for a weekend get-away to Las Vegas or one of those big screen TVs that everyone has these days!

When you compare our $100,000.00 A MONTH SYSTEM to many small businesses – it is dirt cheap! In fact, it is so cheap that many people are <u>SHOCKED</u>!

Yes, many of the people who have been searching for a business that they can own are shocked and amazed when they discover how dirt cheap our $100,000.00 A MONTH SYSTEM is to start! In fact, many of these people are saying, *"This cannot be true! There's no way that you can start a business with all of these advantages for even a fraction of this cost!"*

<u>Most of these people are very skeptical about this</u>. After all, they have been looking at other small businesses that cost as much as $50,000.00 or much, much more! Yes, many small businesses you can start right now will cost you many thousands of dollars – <u>and</u> these businesses do <u>not</u> have the potential to make you rich!

People are spending thousands of dollars to go into all kinds of different businesses that stand almost ZERO chance of making them <u>any</u> significant money.

Want proof?

Okay! *Entrepreneur Magazine* – "the small business authority" – recently put together a list of their top businesses that can be started for the lowest cost. <u>Here is part of that list</u>:

Type of business	Average cost to get started	Average net profit before taxes
Personalized Children's Book	$15,000.00 to $26,000.00	$54,000.00
Medical Claims Processing	$5,000.00 to $17,600.00	$26,500.00
Coffeehouse	$40,000.00 to $60,000.00	$65,000.00
Gift Basket Service	$11,000.00 to $50,000.00	$42,000.00
Auto Detailing	$13,000.00 to $30,000.00	$100,000.00
Wedding Planning Service	$2,700.00 to $13,000.00	$60,000.00

These are some of *Entrepreneur Magazine's* <u>best</u> small businesses that can be started for people who <u>don't</u> have a lot of money to invest.

As you can see, even a simple little business like a small coffee shop is going to cost you $40,000.00 – and you could invest a lot more than that! In fact, I know a man in Newton, Kansas, who told me he invested more than $125,000.00 to start his small "Starbucks" type of coffee house. **Yes, he spent over $125,000.00 before he took in <u>one</u> penny! And guess how much his average coffee sells for?**

$3.25!

Listen. I like this guy and his wife a lot. They have a nice little business and I hope they make it. But he has to sell many tens of thousands of cups of coffee <u>before</u> he'll ever make a profit.

<u>And</u> <u>don't</u> <u>think</u> <u>that</u> <u>this</u> <u>is</u> <u>some</u> <u>kind</u> <u>of</u> <u>isolated</u> <u>story</u>.

<u>It's</u> <u>not</u>! Many people are gladly investing tens – and even hundreds of thousands – of dollars for a wide variety of traditional small businesses that will probably <u>never</u> make them more than $50,000.00 to $75,000.00 a year. And that's <u>if</u> they are lucky. And <u>only</u> after many years of financial struggle.   You would be shocked if you really knew how broke many small businesses are. I was. In many cases these hard-working people are barely able to pay their bills and keep their doors open.

One thing is for sure:

The more you know about the high cost and endless headaches and hassles that most people are going through with <u>most</u> businesses – you will be firmly convinced beyond any doubt that our $100,000.00 A MONTH SYSTEM really is the perfect way to stay home and make money!

How To Instantly Cash-In With The Same System That I'm Using To Reach My Goal Of Making Well Over $500,000 A Month!

This new system is designed to put the largest amount of money in your pocket in the fastest period of time! How fast? Well, I made $10,000.00 cash in my very first week – before I even knew what I was doing!

Will you make $10,000.00 cash in your first week like I did? Well, probably not. After all, I have a great deal of experience in using our powerful Direct Response Marketing methods that have gone into our $100,000.00 A MONTH SYSTEM...

But who knows? You may do <u>even</u> <u>better</u> than I did!

Listen closely. I can't say for sure how much money you will make – but a few things are for certain:

- You'll be cashing in with the same exact System that I'm using to reach my goal of making well over $500,000.00 a month!

- This System is based on the same proven methods that we have perfected and fine-tuned to bring in over $100,000,000.00 in our first 18 years.

- This System combines the <u>best</u> of our multi-million dollar methods – along with the proven secrets that others are already using to make as much as $50,000.00 to $100,000.00 a month!

There are <u>no</u> guarantees or promises as to how much money <u>you</u> <u>will</u> make. No honest and ethical person would <u>ever</u> promise that you <u>will</u> be guaranteed to make any specific sum of money. But the more you know about me – and our proven methods that have generated many tens of millions of dollars for us – and the more you know about the foundational secrets that are making other average people tens of thousands of dollars a month <u>right</u>

away – the more **you will be convinced** that the powerful potential is here for making <u>any</u> amount of money that you really want!

As you really will see – the sky is the limit!

This book will give you my own exciting system that I am using to reach my goal of making over $500,000.00 a month! That's right. This is <u>not</u> a misprint and it's only my targeted goal – but I am shooting for $500,000.00 a month – and firmly believe I will make even more!

That's only my prediction – but once you see how I plan to make well over $500,000.00 a month – and then see how <u>you</u> will use the same exact system that I am using – you will be thrilled!

■ MILLIONAIRE SECRET #53

How to get rich from the comfort, privacy, and security of your own home. You can stay home – watch your favorite TV programs – enjoy time with the people you love – catch all of the cat-naps you want – and <u>still</u> get rich!

This entire System has been built from the ground floor to be done entirely from home!

You will never have to leave your home to cash in big with our powerful $100,000.00 A MONTH SYSTEM! You can stay home each day and enjoy the time with your family – and still make huge sums of money! The only time you'll <u>ever</u> leave home is to deposit the money in your bank. And you don't even have to do that – <u>unless</u> you want!

Yes, you can always mail in your bank deposits if you want!

Being able to make huge sums of money <u>without</u> leaving your home is one of the most thrilling things about our $100,000.00 A

MONTH SYSTEM! This is such an exciting way to make money!

Consider this...

While almost all of your neighbors are forced to jump in their cars every day and put up with all of the hassles of driving through thick traffic to go to a job they hate, you can be making GIANT sums of money from the comfort of your own home! You can watch them drive away in a mad hurry to get to work every day while you relax at the kitchen table with the morning newspaper and a hot cup of coffee!

You can stay home all day – watch your favorite TV programs – enjoy time with the people you love – and catch all of the cat naps you want – and still make a fortune!

Does all this sound like a great fantasy to you?

Something you can only dream of?

Well, it's not!

There are many people living like this every day of the week right now... and YOU can be one of them!

These people are staying home each and every day – relaxing around the house – and <u>still</u> making a fortune!

■ More men fail through lack of purpose than lack of talent.

Billy Sunday

■ Our greatest glory is not in never failing but in rising every time we fall.

Confucius

■ There is nothing like a dream to create the future.

Victor Hugo

One of my best friends loves to get up early each morning just to watch all of his neighbors scramble to work! Some of these people leave every morning when it's still dark and do not get back home until it's dark. They have no time at all for their family and friends. They're killing themselves a little more every day because they hate their jobs and they hate all of the headaches and hassles of traveling to work each day – but they are forced to do it.

You will never have that problem ever again: **Our $100,000.00 A MONTH SYSTEM lets you stay home and relax and <u>still</u> make more money than most people will make working long hours in some unhealthy office environment!** This one advantage alone is enough of a reason for you to jump for joy because you have the courage and vision to invest in this revolutionary moneymaker!

■ **MILLIONAIRE SECRET #54**

The $50,000 An Hour Secret!
How To Quickly Profit From The Same System That Has Made Me As Much As $50,000 In One Hour!

It's possible to make many tens of thousands a month in your spare time! The amount of money you make has <u>nothing</u> to do with the amount of time you put in. You are paid on other things than your time!

This gives you the same powerful secret that the richest people in the world use to make their fortunes! You can put in as little as 10 minutes a day and still be in the powerful position to get paid many thousands of dollars!

I don't blame you if you're skeptical about this – but it's true!

You'll be using the same powerful marketing system that we have been using to make tens of millions of dollars! I have personally used this marketing system for many years to get paid as much as...

$50,000.00 an hour!

Yes, I've used this to make as much as $50,00.00 in one hour! But wait! Don't think I'm bragging. The <u>only</u> reason I'm telling you about our success is because of that fact that <u>you</u> will be using the same marketing system that we've used to make our fortune. I know that if this marketing system has made us millions of dollars – then it has the awesome power to make <u>you</u> a fortune! Yes, you can cash in with the same secret that has made me as much as $50,000 in one hour!

Remember, we simply took our proven marketing system and mixed it with the powerful <u>new</u> secrets that others are using <u>right now</u> to bring in as much as $50,000.00 to $100,000.00 a month! This has created an <u>explosive</u> new opportunity that has the awesome power to make you rich!

So let me go back to my example... Read on and...

I will prove to you that this has the potential power to make you very <u>rich</u>.

As I said, there have been many times when I made over $50,000.00 for the actual work I personally did... **The reason I was able to make over $50,000.00 for one hour is so easy to explain that I'm afraid you may think it's too simple.**

Don't make this mistake...

You see, although this is a simple secret – it really does have the potential power to make you a GIANT fortune.

Here it is...

■ You must find an opportunity that has the potential to pay you huge profits on a valuable item that people really want.

■ Then you simply need a proven marketing system that automatically sells this high-profit product or service for you!

That's it!

These are the two simple steps that you can use to make as much as tens of thousands of dollars in a single hour!

It's a simple formula. But <u>don't</u> be fooled by its simplicity:

Just create or control a highly profitable product or service that people really want. Then build or gain access to a proven marketing system that sells this highly profitable item for you! <u>This</u> <u>is</u> <u>exactly</u> <u>what</u> <u>you</u> <u>are</u> <u>doing</u> <u>when</u> <u>you</u> <u>use</u> <u>this</u> <u>powerful</u> <u>$100,000.00</u> <u>A MONTH SYSTEM</u>!

- There is a huge demand for these very specialized high-ticket items in our $100,000.00 A MONTH SYSTEM! People are spending many <u>billions</u> of dollars right <u>now</u> on similar items.

- And our marketing system is designed to let you sell large numbers of these in-demand items <u>without</u> talking to anyone!

It's like mixing two powerful chemicals together that cause a huge explosion!

■ MILLIONAIRE SECRET #55

FIVE MORE REASONS Why Our Proven System Could Be Worth <u>Millions</u> Of Dollars To You And Your Family!

Remember, the $100,000.00 A MONTH SYSTEM secret that others are using to make $50,000.00 to $100,000.00 a month is fairly new.

<u>But</u> <u>the</u> <u>foundation</u> <u>behind</u> <u>this</u> <u>amazing</u> <u>wealth</u> <u>system</u> <u>is</u> <u>not</u> <u>new</u>.

This is the same marketing system that we have been using since 1988 to bring in many tens of millions of dollars.

Here are FIVE MORE REASONS why our proven system could be worth <u>millions</u> of dollars to you and your family!

    1. It is proven.

    2. It is rock solid.

    3. It has been tested over a long period of time.

    4. All of the bugs have been fully removed.

    5. And, best of all, it is a powerful marketing system that <u>nobody</u> else has!

Yes, this powerful multi-million dollar marketing system is the foundation of our all new $100,000.00 A MONTH SYSTEM!

Best of all, none of the other people who are using the secrets in our $100,000.00 A MONTH SYSTEM have this proven millionaire-making system! This gives <u>you</u> a major advantage over <u>all</u> of them!

But here is one very important detail...

Our $100,000.00 A MONTH SYSTEM was built around the main mistakes that all of the other people who are already using this secret are making.

This is very important! Remember, there are three main mistakes that all of the people who are using this secret are making...

So, here's what we did:

    1. We studied these three major mistakes that all of the people who are already making huge sums of money are making...

    2. We analyzed them carefully.

    3. Then we built our powerful and proven $100,000.00 A MONTH SYSTEM to completely eliminate all 3 of these very glaring mistakes that all of the others are making.

This lets you use the same secret that other average people are using to make tens of thousands of dollars a month – _without_ all of the headaches and hassles!

■ MILLIONAIRE SECRET #56

How Our $100,000 A Month System Works Like A Finely Tuned Money-Machine That Can Crank Out More Money Than You Have <u>Ever</u> Dreamed Of Making!

With our System, you will never talk with a single person, unless you want.

<u>All</u> of the other people who are making thousands a month with this basic secret are doing way too much personal selling.

I hate this!

My company is involved in an area of marketing called: "Direct Response." This powerful form of marketing is responsible for the sale of over 300 billion dollars worth of goods and services each year <u>without</u> any personal selling!

This is the most powerful marketing method on earth! And this is the form of marketing in our revolutionary new $100,000.00 A MONTH SYSTEM!

Direct Response Marketing does an amazing job of selling because...

- It attracts all of the <u>right</u> people and repels the wrong ones.

- It brings all of these people to you automatically!

- It does a powerful job of educating these people on all of the major advantages of your product or service.

■ The first test of a truly great man is his humility.

John Ruskin

■ Nothing grows well in the shade of a big tree.

Constantin Brancusi

■ Men of genius do not excel in any profession because they labor in it, but they labor in it because they excel.

William Hazlitt

■ It eliminates <u>all</u> of their biggest objections...

■ Then it makes them want to buy <u>now</u>!

And best of all, it does all of this without any direct effort on your part!

The sales materials and methods we have built into our $100,000.00 A MONTH SYSTEM do all of the actual selling for you!

These sales materials were designed and built by knowledgeable people who have a long and proven track record for making millions of dollars! They are designed to crank out huge sums of money for you like a well-oiled money machine!

This System gives you such a powerful advantage over all of the other people who are already making tens of thousands of dollars a month with the secrets in this System! Those people are doing a lot of personal selling.

But you won't do any personal selling! In fact, we will show you how it is potentially possible to make many tens of thousands of dollars a month without talking to anyone!

We will be there for you — to help you make the largest

sum of money possible with our powerful marketing system that has been proven to generate many tens of millions of dollars!

Remember, one of the main reasons I am so <u>thrilled</u> about this $100,000.00 A MONTH SYSTEM is because of the simple, but powerful fact that <u>our</u> <u>success</u> <u>is</u> <u>directly</u> <u>tied</u> <u>to</u> <u>your</u> <u>success</u>!

As you know, our #1 goal is to bring in over $500,000.00 a month. But the more you know about our powerful system, the more you will realize that <u>the</u> <u>only</u> <u>way</u> that we can achieve this goal is by doing everything that we can to help you get off to the most powerful and profitable start! The more we do to help you make the largest sum of money in the shortest period of time – the closer we will be to achieving our own goal of making over $500,000.00 a month!

The fact that our success is <u>directly</u> tied to your success is the most powerful benefit that has been built into our amazing $100,000.00 A MONTH SYSTEM.

This gives you the main advantages you would expect from a high-dollar franchise opportunity <u>without</u> spending tens or hundreds of thousands of dollars!

Our $100,000.00 A MONTH SYSTEM is not a franchise. But it does give you some of the most beneficial wealth-making advantages.

In fact, the more I think about this, the more I believe that...

Our $100,000.00 A MONTH SYSTEM is far <u>better</u> and way more powerful than many franchises that sell for up to $500,000.00 or more!

Okay, that's a bold statement and it's only my strong opinion. But when you go over <u>all</u> of the rock-solid reasons <u>why</u> I firmly believe this, I'm betting that **you will be as convinced as I am that in many ways this $100,000.00 A MONTH SYSTEM beats every other opportunity – including those which cost as much as $500,000.00 or even <u>more</u> to start.**

It's a very bold statement. But like everything else I have told you in this book – I will back it up with <u>solid</u> facts that you can sink your teeth into.

This is a long-term opportunity
that can make you super rich!

Our $100,000.00 A MONTH SYSTEM is designed to make you ever-growing amounts of money for the next 10... 20... and even 30 years and beyond! This can be a part of your estate and all of the automatic income you can make is available to your family.

Remember, this revolutionary wealth-making opportunity is a powerful combination of 3 of the hottest multi-billion dollar trends. They are producing billions of dollars right now and <u>the best years</u> are still ahead! Yes, the future is so bright you gotta wear shades!

Listen closely. Although there are <u>no</u> guarantees or promises...

I firmly believe this opportunity stands a greater chance of making you many tens of thousands of dollars month for the next 2 or 3 decades than <u>any other</u> opportunity I have ever seen.

The reason I believe this opportunity can be making you and your family huge sums of money for the next 20 to 30 years and beyond is because of <u>all</u> of the reasons we have talked about <u>added</u> together!

If you have been listening to all of my past audio programs and reading my special reports – you know: There are many different, powerful wealth-making ingredients that have gone into this revolutionary $100,000.00 A MONTH SYSTEM!

It is the explosive combination of <u>all</u> of them working together that has the awesome power to make you massive sums of money for many years!

My favorite combination that creates this synergistic power is...

- The 3 explosive markets behind this new wealth-maker!

- The fact that <u>YOU</u> get paid the largest amount of money and <u>not</u> the company who developed this opportunity.

- The fact that <u>YOU</u> get paid <u>before</u> the company gets paid!

- The fact that I get paid the largest amount of money for doing everything within my power to help you get paid the largest amount of money in the fastest period of time!

- The fact that we have added our own multi-million dollar marketing system to this powerful wealth-making opportunity!

When you mix these five powerful ingredients together, you create a true money-making explosion!

Of course, this list only gives you my TOP-5 WEALTH-MAKING INGREDIENTS. But these 5 are more than enough to give you financial independence for the rest of your life!!!

■ **MILLIONAIRE SECRET #57**

Why It's Possible For You To Get Paid Many Thousands Of Dollars For Doing Very Little Of Anything At All!

Remember, the amount of money you can get paid has <u>nothing</u> to do with the amount of actual time you put in!

Because of this, it is possible...

For you to get paid many thousands of dollars a month for doing very little of anything! It's our powerful and proven System that does all of the work for you!

Our powerful proven system is designed to:

- Attract the people who are most likely to buy all of the high-profit products and services.

- Make all of the sales for you automatically.

- And then pay you huge sums of money for each high-profit transaction that is done for you!

Yes, this system is designed to do it <u>all</u> for you!

Remember, you will be cashing in with the same powerful marketing methods that have brought us tens of millions of automatic dollars!

We have worked very hard since the mid 1980's to perfect our Direct Response Marketing skills and abilities. You will be cashing in from our many years of hard work! Our System does <u>all</u> of this for you! This powerful system is the closest thing to an actual money machine that you will ever find.

We have worked hard to build this system to reach our own goal of making over $500,000.00 a month! This is very important... You'll be plugging into the same exact system that we have built to make millions with this amazing discovery! This gives you tremendous power to make massive profits! You will gain leverage from <u>all</u> of our hard work. You'll have the full power of our many years of wealth-making know-how!

We have a long and successful track record for generating millions of dollars from people who we <u>never</u> meet or even talk with!

Not to brag, but we have taken in over $100,000,000.00 in our first 18 years from our headquarters in rural Kansas. I challenge you to find Goessel, Kansas, on a map! **Here we are in the middle of nowhere — bringing in many millions of dollars a year — with the same system you'll be cashing in with!**

There is no better testament to the money-making power of our amazing Direct Response Marketing methods!

And when you mix our powerful millionaire-making secrets — along with the powerful secrets that are already making other average people many tens of thousands of dollars a month right now — you truly have one of the greatest wealth-making opportunities in history!

■ **MILLIONAIRE SECRET #58**

How to do <u>ONE</u> <u>BASIC</u> <u>STEP</u> To Set Your Money-Machine Into Motion!

Again, at the risk of sounding like pure hype, this is the easiest wealth-making opportunity to start that I have ever seen!

How easy? That's the shocking part... **You see, there is <u>only</u> <u>one</u> <u>basic</u> <u>step</u> for you to take. That's it!** Just one very simple and easy step is all it takes to set our money-making machine into motion!

Think of this easy step as a domino. You simply tip it and knock down a whole line of other dominoes that are in front of it...

This is a good visual. Why? You see, it does take a couple of days to understand everything about this opportunity... There are many things you must know <u>before</u> you can simply tip the one domino and watch all of the others fall down!

Of course, 'THIS SINGLE DOMINO' is only a metaphor to try to illustrate the incredible power behind our $100,000.00 A MONTH SYSTEM. But it's the most powerful visual example!

Now try to imagine a huge pile of 10,000 dominoes...

Let's say that each one of these dominoes represents a key money-making benefit and advantage that has gone into our powerful $100,000.00 A MONTH SYSTEM... <u>You</u> <u>stand</u> <u>them</u> <u>up</u> <u>in</u> <u>a</u> <u>straight</u> <u>line</u>. Then when you get to the end — you have one last domino in your hand.

This final domino is yours alone.

You take this last domino and place in front of the other 9,999. Now you have 10,000 dominoes all standing up on a huge 100-yard football field or basketball court...

Now all you have to do is tip the first domino and all of the rest of the dominoes will automatically tip over!

This is the best metaphor that I can give you to help you understand the awesome power of our $100,000.00 A MONTH SYSTEM! Here's how...

This book tells you a great deal about the powerful ingredients that are built into this $100,000.00 A MONTH SYSTEM so you will fully understand how <u>all</u> of this is designed to make you a fortune.

■ The cards you hold in the game of life mean very little — it's the way you play them that counts.

■ Courage is resistance to fear, mastery of fear — not absence of fear.

Mark Twain

■ Have the courage to act instead of react.

Earlene Larson Jenks

But once you understand all of this – it will only take me 10 minutes to tell you about the one simple and easy step that you will be using! Best of all, this <u>ONE</u> <u>BASIC</u> <u>STEP</u> is all that you need to set your money-machine into motion!

What's so great about this one basic step?

That's simple, but amazingly powerful!

This step is designed to create a powerful chain reaction that causes huge sums of money to come flowing to you! I can't wait to reveal all of the secrets to you!

Two Powerful EXIT STRATEGIES <u>GUARANTEE</u> That You Will <u>Never</u> Have To Worry About Losing Money!

Most people <u>never</u> consider an exit strategy. They think it's negative to ask, "What if something goes wrong?" Or, "What happens if I want out?"

But this is <u>not</u> being negative. It's being smart!

Listen. As I have shown you, this opportunity has the powerful potential to make you financially free for life! **Everything has been set up so that you can make the largest amount of money for the <u>longest</u> period of time – with the least amount of effort.** But there are no guarantees in life and business – and things can and do change. So – although this has been designed to make you tens of thousands of dollars a month for many decades – <u>nobody</u> can ever predict with total certainty what the future will hold.

So it's <u>always</u> smart and <u>never</u> negative to have a back-up plan and an exit strategy. In fact, I firmly believe that having a back-up plan or exit strategy is the most positive and powerful thing that you can do!

After all, once you know beyond any doubt that everything will be okay even if the worst situation occurs, you will be in the most powerful position to move forward with total confidence!

So lets take a look at the two possible exit strategies that you have with our $100,000.00 A MONTH SYSTEM... These are the two powerful EXIT STRATEGIES that <u>GUARANTEE</u> that you will <u>never</u> have to worry about losing money:

<u>Exit Strategy #1</u> – **You will be fully protected if something would ever happen to the company who developed this revolutionary opportunity.**

Remember, the largest amount of money is paid to <u>you</u> and not the company behind this wealth-making discovery.

You get paid the most money – and you are paid <u>first</u>. This puts you in the strongest position!

In fact, in some very important ways, you will be in a more powerful position than the company itself!

After all, you are the first to get paid so – unlike most opportunities – you will <u>never</u> have to wait by the mailbox for your check to arrive. **If something awful would ever happen to the company behind this, you will be okay.** The fact that you are the <u>first</u> to get paid and you make the largest percentage of money puts you in a genuine position of power! **Unlike most opportunities, there is no way this company can <u>ever</u> take your money and run!** This alone gives you a powerful advantage over the millions of people in all kinds of network marketing and other types of distributorships...

So Exit Strategy #1 gives you all of the power!

This puts you in the powerful position to go full blast and make as much money as you can make without the threat of the company cheating you out of any money. This sets you up for the second Exit Strategy.

> **<u>Exit Strategy #2</u> – Once you are free from the fear of being cheated, you can focus on making the largest amount of money.**

Now you can put all of your focus on filling up your bank account with large amounts of cash. And there is no better exit strategy than having lots of money in the bank! Once you have a few million socked away – you will <u>never</u> have another financial worry for the rest of your life!

■ MILLIONAIRE SECRET #60

65 powerful reasons why I firmly believe our proven system really can make you up to $100,000 a month or a whole lot more!

On the next few pages, you will discover the 65 Amazing

Reasons Why I Believe That You Could Make Up to $100,000 A Month <u>Without</u> Multi-Level Marketing... These reasons are broke down into these FIVE categories:

CATEGORY#1: You will discover the 15 main reasons why the $100,000.00 A MONTH SYSTEM has the power to make you rich!

CATEGORY #2: You will discover our 12-QUESTION <u>ACID TEST</u> <u>FORMULA</u> that we use to separate the programs that can make you millions of dollars from all of the others... and why our $100,000.00 A MONTH SYSTEM passes with flying colors!

CATEGORY #3: You will discover our 5 Magic Keys To Wealth That Have The Power To Make You A Millionaire In No Time Flat! <u>You will discover what these 5 keys are and how each one of them has been built into this opportunity</u>.

CATEGORY #4: You will also receive the 27-key advantages THAT SEPARATE OUR $100,000.00 A MONTH SYSTEM from the other opportunities that we research!

And last, but not least...

CATEGORY #5: You will discover how Our $100,000.00 A Month System lets you cash in with each one of the six ingredients you need to get rich!

Add it up. You'll see. These are the 65 reasons why this is the perfect way for you to stay home and make huge sums of money!

The 15 Main Reasons Why Our System Has the Power to Make You Rich!

1.   **The timing is perfect for this amazing discovery!**
     Unlike most opportunities "claiming" to be in a new market, our new $100,000.00 A MONTH SYSTEM allows you to cash-in with not one, but three emerging multi-billion dollar markets in a whole new way.

2.   **Many are making huge mistakes and <u>still</u> getting rich!**

We've identified and eliminated 3 serious mistakes that others are making and we believe that these will allow our Clients to succeed even further.

3. **You can get huge sums of daily cash that comes to you super fast!** This amazing discovery is designed to pay you huge sums of money early and often and best of all you get paid before the company.

4. **You can also get paid giant sums of residual income every month!** This steady and predictable income builds into a dependable stream that can grow bigger and bigger.

5. **WE CAN DO <u>EVERYTHING</u> FOR YOU!** As a valuable member of our team, our success is tied to your success and so we'll do everything that we can to help!

6. **We have discovered a whole new way to make money with this proven secret (that's <u>already</u> making other people up to $100,000.00 a month)!** This gives you many powerful advantages based on powerful wealth-making discoveries that have already made us tens of millions of dollars!

7. **You will cash-in with our powerful system that <u>none</u> of the people who are <u>already</u> making many thousands of dollars a month have or can use!** Whether you do it by yourself or have us do everything for you this millionaire-making system that we have developed can <u>only</u> be used by <u>you</u> and the group of others we bring into this opportunity!

8. **We have <u>THE</u> <u>ULTIMATE</u> <u>REASON</u> to help you get paid the largest sum of cash — in the fastest time!** I CAN GET VERY RICH — BY DOING EVERYTHING POSSIBLE TO HELP <u>YOU</u> GET OFF TO A FAST AND EASY START AND GET PAID THE LARGEST SUM OF MONEY RIGHT AWAY!

9. **This is designed to pay you up to thousands of dollars within days!** Yes, I made ten thousand dollars in my first week (before I knew what I was doing) so I am proof that this

can make you huge sums of fast cash!

10. **You make all of your money in total privacy!** Be in the powerful position that 99% of all other people can only dream of: <u>Never</u> have to talk with or personally sell anything to anyone!

11. **The same people who have made us millions of dollars can do <u>everything</u> for you!** YOU CAN LITERALLY GET THE SAME PEOPLE WORKING FOR YOU WHEN WE DO EVERYTHING FOR YOU, *even use the same expert suppliers and service providers we use!!!*

12. **You'll have an almost unfair advantage over all of the people who are already getting rich with this opportunity!** Unlike all of the other people who are making thousands of dollars, with our System you'll be able to reach all of the skeptical people who are perfect candidates for this amazing opportunity.

13. **ALL OF THE MONEY COMES <u>STRAIGHT</u> TO YOU!** You'll <u>never</u> worry if the International company behind this opportunity is paying you every single penny of your money.** You get paid <u>before</u> the company who developed this discovery and what's more you get paid by far the largest sum of money!

14. **The market is <u>still</u> untapped! This is <u>still</u> the ground floor!** Tens of millions of people have <u>never</u> heard of this and we have a proven way to reach this huge group of hot prospects!

15. **This unique wealth-making system contains 27-key advantages THAT SEPARATE IT from almost all other business opportunities that we research every single month!** All you have to do to make a lot of money is to discover our $100,000.00 A MONTH SYSTEM and you'll see that this is better than <u>all</u> of the other opportunities with these 27 problems.

Our 12 Question Acid Test Formula!

#1: **Are average people <u>already</u> making huge sums of money?**
Answer: Yes! Average people are making as much as $50,000.00 to $100,000.00 a month right now!

#2: **Can the opportunity be started for <u>less</u> money than most people can scrape together for something they really want?**
Answer: Yes! You can get started for <u>less</u> than you'd spend for a weekend get-away to Las Vegas or one of those big screen TVs everyone seems to have these days!

#3: **Is it possible to make many thousands of dollars right away?**
Answer: Yes. This system is designed to put the largest amount of money in your pocket in the fastest period of time!

#4: **Can everything be done from the comfort, privacy, and security of your home?**
Answer: "<u>YES!</u>" You can make huge sums of money without leaving home!

■ Few audiences object to a good, short speech, but all will resent a waste of time. Length does not make a speech memorable or effective. The Gettysburg Address, after all was only 269 words. If you have successfully communicated a maximum of three points in a speech, you have done well. Try to communicate too many points, and it's possible — in fact, probable — that your audience will remember none of them clearly.

Finally, a great way to undo the effects of a wonderful and rousing speech is to exceed your allotted time or to keep talking after you've covered the given topic.

#5: **Can someone make huge sums of money in their spare time?**
Answer: YES! It's possible to make many tens of thousands a month in your spare time!

#6: **Is it potentially possible to make millions of dollars?**
Answer: YES! YES! YES! You will be using the same system that we have developed to reach our goal of making over $500,000.00 a month!

#7: **Can you make huge sums of money with <u>no</u> personal selling?**
Answer: Absolutely! You have the potential power to make thousands of dollars a month *without talking with anyone.*

#8: **Is there help, support, and guidance available from experts with a <u>proven</u> <u>track</u> <u>record</u> of making millions of dollars?**
Answer: <u>YES!</u> We will help you make the largest sum of money possible with our powerful marketing system that has been proven to generate tens of millions of dollars!

#9: **Is this a long-term opportunity?**
Answer: Yes, it is! Our $100,000.00 A MONTH SYSTEM is designed to pay you and your family an ever-growing sum of money for many years!

#10: **Can it produce automatic income?**
Answer: Yes, the money can keep flowing to you without <u>any</u> direct effort!

#11: **Is it easy to start?**
Answer: "YES!" I have researched thousands of different business opportunities since 1988 and have <u>never</u> seen an easier opportunity to start!

#12: **Is there an exit strategy in case something goes wrong or you want out?**
Answer: YES! There are <u>two</u> very important exit strategies for you to consider.

Our 5 Magic Keys to Wealth!

1. **There must be an established and growing market for the business you get into.** The market demand for this kind of product and service is strong so the stage is set for many people like you and me to make millions!

2. **You must offer something new or different that sets you apart from all of the other competitors.** These type products and services that can make you a millionaire in no time flat are <u>new</u> and exciting items that fill some type of serious problem in the marketplace.

3. **You must have a strong answer for the skeptical people in the market.** We have <u>A</u> <u>VERY</u> <u>SOLID</u> <u>ANSWER</u> to ease the fears of all the skeptical people and this is just <u>one</u> of the major advantages you will have.

4. **You must build residual income into your entire business plan.** You will discover how my $100,000.00 A MONTH SYSTEM is designed to pay you HUGE sums of upfront cash very quickly and a growing stream of residual income that can keep growing <u>bigger</u> and <u>never</u> stop!

5. **The slack adjuster.** *(A high-ticket item that pays you huge profits.)* The apparent value of our products and services is super high, but thanks to the miracle of technology the actual cost to deliver these items is low! Because of this, there's always plenty of money left over to pay yourself!

27 Key Advantages Our $100,000 A MONTH SYSTEM Has Over All Of The Other Opportunities We've Researched!

1. **Most <u>new</u> opportunities are totally unproven.**
Our $100,000.00 A MONTH SYSTEM is the greatest discovery ever for cashing in with three multi-billion dollar markets that are already generating a fortune and getting ready to explode with growth!

2. **Most of the money-making methods are the same boring plans and programs *that will never make you rich.*** This really is new, different, and better than all of the other opportunities! Plus, it's rock solid in every way.

3. **Most money-making programs only make the promoters rich.** Our $100,000.00 A MONTH SYSTEM is designed from the ground up to put the <u>largest</u> amount of money into your pocket in the fastest period of time, with the least amount of effort!

4. **Many of the most exciting ways to make money are either illegal or immoral.** Our $100,000.00 A MONTH SYSTEM is a powerful combination of 3 multi-billion dollar markets that are already producing hundreds of billions of dollars a year without violating any laws or ethics.

5. **Most opportunities are here today and gone tomorrow.** Our $100.000.00 A MONTH SYSTEM is built on solid products with very high-perceived values and are all part of a multi-billion dollar marketplace that is growing by leaps and bounds!

6. **Most opportunities have no way to help you make huge sums of money.** With this amazing System – we are there for you every step of the way. Remember, we earn our biggest profits by helping you get off to a powerful start.

7. **Many opportunity promoters take your money and run.** This opportunity lets <u>you</u> make the largest amount of money and you get paid first, even <u>before</u> the company behind this discovery gets their money!

8. **Most opportunities <u>force</u> you to work long hours with little pay.** Our $100,000.00 A MONTH SYSTEM has been built from the ground floor to make you the largest amount of money in the shortest time and it pays you huge sums of fast cash for very small efforts!

9. **Many opportunities offer products and services that nobody wants.** Other people are already making many billions of dollars with similar types of products and services,

but our items are totally unique and new!

10. **Most business opportunities force you to become a salesperson.** Our Marketing System introduces the valuable products and services to your prospects and then does a complete job of selling for you!

11. **Most opportunities pay you small sums of money and <u>no</u> residual income.** You can get large sums of money paid to you for high-ticket, in-demand products and services that people actually want and need. Plus, there is an automatic residual income built into this $100,000.00 A MONTH SYSTEM!

12. **Most opportunities are not timely.** Our $100,000.00 A MONTH SYSTEM is the timeliest opportunity that I have ever seen since the worldwide web caused the Internet to explode back in 1994.

13. **Many opportunities are too complicated for the average person.** All you have to do is gain full control over a very specialized product or service that others have spent many years to develop. That's it!

14. **Most opportunities <u>cannot</u> be done from the comfort, privacy, and safety of your home.** Our $100,000.00 A MONTH SYSTEM lets you make big money from the comfort and privacy of your own home and has <u>nothing</u> to do with the number of hours you put in.

15. **Most opportunities are <u>very</u> difficult to start and run.** Our amazing new $100,000.00 A MONTH SYSTEM gives you many of the same advantages that a high-dollar franchise gives you, <u>without</u> investing hundreds of thousands of dollars.

16. **Most opportunities do not let you make money fast enough.** Our marketing system is designed to let you deposit the largest amount of cash in the fastest time – with the least effort!

17. **Most opportunities are too alike. They all try hard to copy each other.** This is totally unique from every other

opportunity on the market and it really eliminates all of the problems that are built into many other opportunities that I've researched since 1988.

18. **Most of the opportunities we research are nothing more than hype and B.S.** Our $100,000.00 A MONTH SYSTEM has passed all of my hardest tests with flying colors! It has a large and growing market, something unique that sets it apart, and a marketing system that does some or all of the selling!

19. **Most opportunities are not part of a growing trend.** Good news for you, because our $100,000.00 A MONTH SYSTEM is a multi-billion dollar wave that is still small enough to ride in for major wealth!

20. **Most opportunities are not unique.** This opportunity has such exciting things about it that it keeps you up at night and gets you out of bed in the morning ready to go!

21. **Most opportunities force you to do everything on your own.** With our $100,000.00 A MONTH SYSTEM we are there for you every step of the way.

22. **Most business opportunities will never make you rich!** There are average people who are already making as much as $50,000.00 to $100,000.00 a month with just the basic secrets in our $100,000.00 A MONTH SYSTEM!

23. **Most money-making opportunities do not pay you the largest percentage of upfront cash.** This powerful new system gives you some of the greatest benefits of network marketing without the terrible side effects. You get the largest sum of money paid directly to you first, before the company gets paid!

24. **Most business opportunities are filled with gaps and missing pieces.** This is complete in every way, there are no gaps or missing pieces.

25. **Most business opportunities are LOADED with problems, pain, and frustration.** Our $100,000.00 A MONTH SYSTEM

gives you the ultimate way to stay home and make money <u>without</u> all of the many headaches and hassles that most people are forced to go through!

26. **Most business opportunities require huge sums of money to get started.** I spend 95% of my time researching low-cost business opportunities and I have discovered a unique opportunity that can be started for well under $10,000.00 and has the powerful potential to bring in millions every year!

27. **Most business opportunities are very risky.** We have discovered a home-based wealth-making method that eliminates all of the headaches and hassles that most people are forced to go through and gives you the potential to make tens of thousands of dollars a month!

■ Soon after a hard decision something inevitably occurs to cast doubt. Holding steady against that doubt usually proves that decision.

R. I. Ritzhenry

■ We know what happens to people who stay in the middle of the road. They get run over.

Aneurin Bevan

■ The best way out is always through.

Robert Frost

The 6 Powerful Ingredients That You Need to Get Rich!

1. **Many average people <u>must</u> already be making huge sums of money!** This unique opportunity combines 3 multi-billion dollar emerging markets. The best years are still ahead!

2. **You must be able to do everything part-time — from the comfort, privacy, and security of your own home.** Our $100,000.00 A MONTH SYSTEM lets you make money

without having to spend all of your time doing all of the things that 99% of other businesspeople are <u>forced</u> to do! Everything is done for you!

3. **The markets for your products and services must be <u>HUGE</u> and growing quickly! There must be a genuine demand for the items you offer.** Many average people have caught THE BILLION-DOLLAR WAVE and then rode it in for major wealth! Now you can do this, too!

4. **The items being offered must be high-ticket products and services that pay you the largest sum of money for the smallest number of transactions.** Our proven marketing system offers items that have great perceived value to the people who badly want and need them, but the actual cost to distribute them over the Internet is amazingly low!

5. **You must have the help, support, and guidance of people who truly understand how to turn small sums of money into a huge fortune! These people must earn the bulk of their money by doing everything that they can to help you get rich!** With our $100,000.00 A MONTH SYSTEM – we have the ultimate incentive to do <u>all</u> that we can to help you make the largest sum of money in the fastest period of time because that's where the bulk of our profits come from!

6. **You must have a marketing system that does all of the selling for you.** Our powerful $100,000.00 A MONTH SYSTEM makes money for you... automatically! This system has been built from the ground up to sell to the growing number of skeptical people in the market place.

■ **MILLIONAIRE SECRET #61**

The "Bill Gates Billionaire Secret" We Use To Help You Get Started Fast And Make The Largest Sum Of Money From Day One!

As you'll see, our ONE-STEP Marketing System is so easy to understand and use that a 12-year-old child can make money with it! Because of this, it only takes a little time to explain this to you.

The fact that this ONE-STEP Marketing System is simple to understand and use is a great thing for you!

Why?

That's simple: This lets you get off to the most powerful and profitable start. You can get started fast and have the power of momentum working for you from day one!

This is especially important because...

Most marketing plans are very complicated.

The most successful multi-million dollar marketing plans can take a long time to learn. They are difficult to set up and run. This makes it hard for you to get off to a powerful start.

Bill Gates, one of the world's most famous billionaires, says: "If you can't write your basic business and marketing plan on a single sheet of paper – *I WON'T DO IT!*"

This man understands the secret. So do we!

Simplicity is power! The simpler something is, the easier it is to get started and succeed.

Our ONE-STEP Marketing System is simple and easy... And yes, we have put it all on one single sheet of paper. This lets you cash in with the "Bill Gates Billionaire Secret" from day one!

BUT THERE'S ONE MAJOR PROBLEM.

HERE IT IS: On the surface, this one-step system seems way too simple and easy. There is a danger that you will think it's too simple and you will not value or appreciate all of the hard work that it took for us to carefully build this for you.

So let's take some time and tell you about all of the elements that have gone into this very powerful, but simple ONE STEP system. It's important to know about these things. Otherwise, you'll <u>never</u> fully understand and appreciate this powerful system.

So please read carefully. And consider this: ***"The <u>why</u> is always more important than the <u>how</u>!"***

The dictionary defines "<u>why</u>" as the cause or reason behind something. The word "<u>how</u>" is the way you do something.

The most brilliant thinkers have told us that the *why* to do something is always more important than *how* to do it. So let's spend some quality time talking about the different elements that have gone into this powerful ONE-STEP Marketing System. Shall we?

OKAY, for starters...

Think of this ONE-STEP MARKETING SYSTEM as if it were a true money machine that you can use to crank out large amounts of cash whenever you want!

This machine has been carefully built for you. Now all you have to do is punch one button to crank out the money!

The 'money machine' is a great analogy for our $100,000.00 A MONTH SYSTEM. Why? Because this entire Program has been built to let us do all of the complicated things that must be done to crank out the largest amount of sales and profits. However, all you do is one step! This is a simple step and it's so easy to do – but it is such a vital step...

You must know just how important this step is <u>before</u> you can fully appreciate it.

So, here we go!

First, here's a quote from one of my mentors who helped me become a millionaire:

> ***"Marketing takes a day to learn
> and a lifetime to master."***

This is so true!

You see, there are only two basic steps to <u>every</u> great marketing plan:

<u>Step One</u>: Attracting the very best prospects for whatever you are offering.

<u>Step Two</u>: All of the activities that you must go through to sell the largest number of these people the things they really want.

That's it! This is the essence of all marketing! It's simply doing all of the things that you can to attract the very best prospects, sell them, and make sure that they stay happy.

You'll use our ONE STEP MARKETING SYSTEM to take care of the <u>first</u> step. We take care of the second step! **Best of all, our powerful sales materials and our staff do <u>all</u> of the work for you!** Plus, I will show you how to stay home and let the same suppliers that we use take care of this one very important step for you. You'll be thrilled when you realize how easy this is!

■ MILLIONAIRE SECRET #62

Why This Is The Ultimate Wealth-Making Partnership Between Our Company And You!

Don't let the ease and simplicity of the one step that you'll be doing with our '$100,000 A MONTH SYSTEM!' fool you. You will be playing a vital role in our 2-step marketing process. The step you do is vital to your success and ours. All of the basics behind this will be totally clear by the time you finish going through this book. By the end of this book, you will be so excited because you will have a deeper understanding and appreciation of <u>all</u> of the various marketing elements that have gone into this very simple system.

So <u>relax</u>! You may only want to know the "<u>how</u>" to do it part of our system, but the "<u>why</u>" it works is much more important. The more you know about the <u>why</u> it works, the more successful you will be.

Here are the 2 MAIN REASONS <u>why</u> this ONE-STEP Marketing System is the ultimate way to make money:

1. This is built on proven Direct Response Marketing methods that have made us tens of millions of dollars.

2. The one step that you do is vital to <u>both</u> of us! This lets me put <u>all</u> of my company's time and energy into the second step which is made up of all of the things that must be done to sell the new prospects that you will be attracting and to make sure that they stay happy...

As you will see, letting YOU focus on doing the first step — with us putting our time and attention on the second step — is the ultimate win/win partnership between you and my company.

Here are 5 major advantages for you to consider:

1. All you do is one step.
This one step sets everything in motion. Best of all, the same suppliers that we use to build our multi-million dollar company can do this one step for you!

2. The sales materials, our expert staff, and our trusted suppliers do all of the work for you!

3. You will <u>never</u> do any personal selling or even talk with a single person.

4. Our success is directly tied to your success!
We are in the powerful position to make many thousands of dollars for doing all that we can to help you deposit large sums of money into your bank account! We get paid HUGE profits up-front for the help that we give you right away. Plus, we get a small percentage of on-going profits for every dollar that we help you make.

5. This gives you <u>many</u> powerful advantages that the people who are already making thousands of dollars a month don't have!

> ■ A problem is a chance for you to do your best.
>
>   *Duke Ellington*
>
> ■ Problems are only opportunities in work clothes.
>
>   *Henry J. Kaiser*
>
> ■ Some people not only expect opportunity to knock, they expect it to beat the door down.
>
> ■ Gray skies are just clouds passing over.
>
>   *Duke Ellington*

Add it up. You'll see. These five advantages give you the ultimate way to stay home and make huge sums of money!

Now listen carefully...

Our ONE-STEP Marketing System was inspired by the brilliant company behind this revolutionary wealth-making discovery!

This company gave us THE ULTIMATE INCENTIVE to help you get off to the most powerful start! They have given us the opportunity to make LARGE sums of money for the help we give you, to help you make the maximum amount of money in the minimum amount of time, with the least amount of headaches and hassles!

■ **MILLIONAIRE SECRET #63**

The 3-Step Formula That You Can Use RIGHT NOW To Make A Fast Fortune!

Getting rich is very simple. In fact, it's so simple that most people over-think it and will <u>never</u> become financially independent.

You don't have to be one of these people.

Here is the 3-step formula that you can use to get rich:

1. Find average people who are making huge amounts of money.

2. Learn all of their secrets. Do whatever you can to find out what they're doing right and wrong.

3. Then duplicate their actions. Just do more of the things that they're doing right and develop a powerful solution to eliminate each of the major mistakes that they're making.

That's it!

This is the simple 3-step formula that can make you a fast fortune!

The world's most expensive marketing expert (Jay Abraham) taught me this important wealth principle:

"All you have to do to make a fortune is discover a group of people who are already getting rich in spite of making some really stupid mistakes."

That's <u>how</u> we developed our $100,000 A MONTH SYSTEM:

<u>STEP ONE:</u>   A friend of mine told me about a group of average people who were making tens of thousands of dollars a month. Some of them were making as much as $50,000.00 to $100,000.00 a month!

<u>STEP TWO:</u>   My staff and I discovered what these people were doing to make their huge monthly fortunes. We found out what they were doing right and wrong.

<u>STEP THREE:</u> Then, we simply developed a powerful marketing system around the 3 biggest mistakes that all of the successful people were making.

<u>This</u> <u>is</u> <u>so</u> <u>great,</u> <u>I</u> <u>must</u> <u>say</u> <u>it</u> <u>again</u>...

Our ONE-STEP Marketing System was built around the three biggest mistakes that other people who are already making thousands of dollars a month are making right now. As you will see, we have eliminated each mistake in a very powerful way.

■ MILLIONAIRE SECRET #64

How To Make A Fortune With The Same "SLOW-SELLING METHOD" That Has Made Us Millions!

Tens of millions of people are searching for a proven way to make huge sums of money. This is good news for you because our '$100,000 A MONTH SYSTEM!' is a powerful way to cash in from this lucrative marketplace of people who are desperately searching for a proven way to stay home and make money... All you have to do is figure out a legitimate way to help them get what they want and <u>you</u> can become very rich!

It sounds simple. And it really can be.

After all, the world's greatest success coach (Zig Ziglar) says: *"You can have anything you want if you will only help enough other people get what <u>they</u> want."*

Zig is right!

We have brought in tens of millions of dollars by doing everything possible to help the people in the opportunity market. These people are <u>desperate</u> for a proven way to get rich. Now you have the potential power to make a fortune helping them, just like we have.

But there's one major problem standing in your way: It's the simple, but often ignored fact that...

These people are very skeptical.

There are so many lies and misleading information about all of the business opportunities that claim to be "the next BIG thing."

There are too many scams that lead to one dead-end after another.

Can you relate to this? If so, you are very typical of all of the people in the opportunity market who have been lied to and cheated so many times that you're leery of <u>almost</u> <u>everything</u> you see and hear...

But most people who promote business opportunities want to bury their heads in the sand and pretend these problems don't exist:

- They have no answers for all of the skeptical people. They offer no solution to this major problem. They ignore it and pretend it doesn't exist.

- They try to sell these skeptical people too much, too fast. And the best prospects run away and never turn back for another look.

This is a major mistake that you will never make when you use our '$100,000 A MONTH SYSTEM!' You will be cashing in with our "SLOW-SELLING METHOD" that has made us millions! This is a proven set of methods that we will use on your behalf to make it easy for skeptical people to NEVER feel pressured in any way, shape, or form. I'll cover this in more detail in the next Millionaire Secret. *Read on...*

■ **MILLIONAIRE SECRET #65**

Why Getting Super Rich Is <u>Not</u> A Numbers Game.

Business opportunity promoters say things like; *"It's all a numbers game."* And it is, if what you have to offer is pure crap...

But if what you have to offer can really help people make huge sums of money, then you're doing them a disservice by <u>not</u> doing everything you can to introduce them to your opportunity a bit slower. When you have something totally legitimate, it's <u>not</u> *"a numbers game"* – it's *"a*

relationship game."

THE BOTTOM LINE: The people who are already making a fortune with the basic secrets in this system are scaring away the best prospects. They have no real answer for all of the skepticism in the marketplace. They're trying to "sell" to people instead of letting them learn more about the opportunity at their own pace.

Our ONE-STEP Marketing System eliminates this major mistake:

- We make people feel that they are choosing us rather than us chasing after them.

- **WE EDUCATE THEM SLOWLY.** We don't tell them too much too fast. We place a high value on their skepticism and let them discover all of the secrets at their own pace instead of making them feel high-pressured.

- We treat this as *'a relationship game,'* not *'a numbers game.'* This sets us apart from all of the other people who are scaring the best prospects away.

Our ONE STEP MARKETING SYSTEM attracts, not repels. We educate people slowly. **We have a solid answer for their doubts and fears.** And we let people come to us and feel empowered by the choices that they make. There is <u>never</u> any high-pressure. This makes it easier for us to help you make the largest sum of money with our '$100,000 A MONTH SYSTEM!'

■ MILLIONAIRE SECRET #66

Why You Should <u>Never</u> Fear The Competition.

Marketing is all about *differentiation*. It's setting yourself apart from the other companies who are doing everything that they can to command the attention and interest of the same prospects that you are trying to attract.

CONSIDER THIS: The people who make millions of dollars

find ways to completely separate themselves from all of the other companies in the marketplace. We spend a great deal of time and money to discover the weak points in our competitors' armor!

That sounds like a military metaphor, doesn't it? Well...

Marketing can be a lot like warfare!

Your competitors (with a few golden exceptions) are the enemy! These people are trying to take away the money that could and should be yours!

Does that sound ruthless? It's not, <u>if</u> what you're offering is truly legitimate in every way.

Listen closely. Many people make some very serious mistakes when it comes to the subject of competition. They either minimize it and pretend it doesn't exist or they blow it way out of proportion and become overly frightened and threatened by it.

You cannot make these mistakes! Do not turn a blind eye to the competition. They are out there trying to attract the same people you are trying to attract. Be aware of this, but...

<u>Never</u> fear the competition.

You can learn a lot by keeping your eyes wide open. Study the competition. Learn from them. Ask yourself, *"What are they doing right and wrong?"* And the most important question: *"What can I do to completely separate myself from all of these other people?"*

These are the questions that we asked ourselves when we investigated <u>all</u> of the people who are already making GIANT sums of money with the secrets in our $100,000.00 A MONTH SYSTEM.

The answers to these questions became the solutions that you will now have when you use our powerful ONE-STEP Marketing System! We have discovered a simple way to completely separate ourselves from <u>all</u> of the other individuals in the business opportunity market – and from <u>all</u> of the people who are already using the basic secrets in our $100,000 A MONTH SYSTEM! This gives you a powerful advantage that none of these people have. You can use this advantage to make <u>HUGE</u> sums of money!

■ MILLIONAIRE SECRET #67

PERSONAL SELLING SUCKS!
Here Are The 4 Reasons You Should <u>HATE</u> Personal Selling And <u>LOVE</u> Our One-Step System That Does <u>All</u> The Selling For You!

Let me be very clear about the whole subject of personal selling: <u>I HATE IT</u>! And so do most of my friends and clients...

Here are the 4 main reasons:

(1) We hate the rejection of personal selling.

(2) We are sick and tired of all of the things that we have to do to persuade other people to buy what we sell.

(3) We hate answering and endless series of objections.

(4) We hate intruding on other people.

THE BOTTOM LINE: All of us hate the pushiness of high-

■ He that is good for making excuses is seldom good for anything else.

Benjamin Franklin

■ If you let other people do it for you, they will do it to you.

Robert Anthony

■ The speed of the leader is the speed of the pack.

Yukon saying

---

pressure sales people. We hate the manipulation of aggressive salespeople who try to manipulate us into giving them our money. We hate being "sold."

Listen closely...

Personal selling is the most terrible way to make money.

I did a lot of personal selling when I was younger, because I wanted to make good money and didn't have a college education. **I've faced all of the pain and suffering of having hundreds of doors slammed in my face!** I've been hung up on thousands of times. I've been yelled at and cursed at. I've suffered from all kinds of terrible humiliation from all of the rejection.

But I didn't know there was a better way...

HERE'S MY QUICK STORY: My friend, Ron Sheppeard, hired me as a salesperson in 1984. Before that, I was a welder in a factory. Ron knew I wanted more out of life and thought I'd make a good salesperson. He hired me, coached me, and gave me a lot of books to read and tapes to listen to.

It was a great, but painful education.

Becoming a salesperson led me to start my first business in December of 1985. I will <u>always</u> be grateful for that. But the only way I knew how to promote my company was to knock on doors and call people on the phone. Because of this, I've had thousands of doors slammed in my face and have been hung up on thousands of times. But I didn't know that there was any better way to build my business...

Then in 1988 my wife, Eileen, and I discovered the awesome power of Direct Response Marketing and our lives were changed forever!

This is a powerful form of marketing that does <u>all</u> of the selling for you:

■ There is zero rejection!

- You can sell to tens of thousands, and even millions, of people without talking to anyone!

- The sales material and the methods you lump together in your marketing system do <u>all</u> of the selling for you!

- The only people you <u>ever</u> hear from are those who say *"<u>Yes</u>!"*

Direct Response Marketing is a little-known method that's responsible for over 300 billion dollars a year in total revenue. Yes, hundreds of billions are generated each year thanks to this powerful form of marketing. And yet, it remains virtually unknown to most businesspeople and entrepreneurs... But you won't be one of them! Read on...

■ MILLIONAIRE SECRET #68

The Power Of "STEALTH MARKETING" ...And How Our System Lets You Use It To Get Super Rich!

So why don't more people know about the exciting wealth-making method?

That's simple. You see, good Direct Response Marketing is what I call: *"STEALTH MARKETING."* It's like those fighter jets that remain undetected by radar. It's hard to spy on the people who are making millions in Direct Response and discover all of their hidden secrets.

This brings me to some good and bad news:

<u>*THE BAD NEWS*</u>:

Direct Response Marketing can be very deceptive. On the surface, it seems so simple and it really can be when you have all of the right elements in place... But underneath the surface there are many different strategies and methods that are responsible for the billions of dollars that are being generated each year. These more advanced methods <u>remain hidden from the view of the novice</u> who thinks or is led to believe that this is a simple and easy way to get rich.

<u>AND NOW FOR THE GOOD NEWS</u>: We have taken all of the best-of-the-best of our Direct Response Marketing secrets that have brought us over $100-MILLION DOLLARS in *less* than 18 years and built them into our ONE STEP MARKETING SYSTEM that's designed to make you huge sums of money from the comfort of your own home!

Here are 5 MAIN REASONS why our $100,000.00 A MONTH SYSTEM has the ability to make you tens of thousands of dollars a month:

1. It lets you tap into the awesome wealth-making power of Direct Response Marketing!

2. It is based on proven methods that have made us tens of millions of dollars.

3. We have built it for you and can run your entire business for you. **Yes, we can do everything for you!** All you do is fill out a couple of forms and mail them out when the money comes in. That's it. We can take care of everything else.

4. **This is a truly duplicatable wealth-making system.** This is the same system that we're using to reach our goal of bringing in over $500,000.00 a month. You can use it, too! Plus, all of the people we place on your team can also use it to make money for you. (More on this, later).

5. It gives you an unfair advantage over all of the other people who are already making many thousands of dollars a month!

Remember, this Marketing System completely eliminates <u>all 3</u> of the major mistakes that everyone else is making:

<u>**Solution for Mistake #1**</u> — It attracts the best prospects instead of

repelling them.

Solution for Mistake #2 — It does an amazing job of separating <u>you</u> from all of the other competitors.

Solution for Mistake #3 — It does a complete job of selling for you! You will <u>never</u> talk with anyone!

Our $100,000.00 A MONTH SYSTEM is a powerful intermediate step that absorbs your marketing costs and generates high quality leads.

This lets you tap into the power of 2-step marketing:
<u>STEP ONE:</u> It attracts the highest quality prospects <u>only</u> and repels all of the others. **<u>STEP TWO:</u>** It sells the largest percentage of these prospects for the maximum profit possible.

But wait, there's more!

Yes, there's ONE MORE IMPORTANT STEP that's built into our System that has the awesome power to make you a millionaire in <u>no time flat</u>! <u>HERE IT IS:</u> We make it super easy to let other people use our same exact turn-key system to make a fortune for you! This is brilliant!

■ **MILLIONAIRE SECRET #69**

How To Let Up To Thousands Of People Make Money For You...
 <u>Without</u> Multi-Level Marketing!

Our $100,000 A MONTH SYSTEM gives you the ultimate way to let up to hundreds, or perhaps thousands, of other people make money for you!

These people (who we place on your team) can use the same powerful ONE-STEP Marketing System that we have built for you. I will show you <u>how</u> all of this works later... And you will be thrilled when you understand how all of this is designed to make you a fortune!

When you completely understand everything that has gone into this powerful $100,000 A MONTH SYSTEM you will be speechless! This really is the most powerful home-based wealth-maker in the world.

Why? Well, it all boils down to one major advantage:

It gives you the same advantages as the world's richest people enjoy!

CONSIDER THIS: The world's richest people make money on <u>many</u> things that have nothing to do with the amount of time and work they actually do. They make money from the efforts of other people, from the sale of certain products or services, or from other income producing assets that let them sit back and let their money make more money for them.

Yes, these wealthy people have many ways to continue to earn a fortune, even when they do nothing. Now you can enjoy these same powerful advantages.

■ **MILLIONAIRE SECRET #70**

The Wealth-Making Power Of Passive Income... And How Our System Lets You Cash-In With It Right Now!

As I am about to show you, there are only 3 ways to make money.

Here they are:

MONEY-MAKING METHOD #1:

You can sell your time for money.

This is the way 99% of the people make almost all of their money. Everyone from day laborers, who slave under the hot sun for minimum wage, to brain surgeons who get paid thousands of dollars an hour. All of these people are selling their time for money.

MONEY-MAKING METHOD #2:

**You can sell a product or service
or combination of both.**

With this second method, your money comes from the sale of some product or service, <u>not</u> the amount of time you work. **This is a much smarter way to make money!** In fact, the world is filled with many millionaires who make almost all of their money with this second powerful method.

■ The tragedy of life doesn't lie in not reaching your goal. The tragedy lies in having no goal to reach.

Benjamin E. Mays

■ It is a funny thing about life: if you refuse to accept anything but the best you very often get it.

W. Somerset Maugham

■ Quality is not an act. It is a habit.

Aristotle

But the real secret to getting rich is to use the final method.

Just look...

MONEY-MAKING METHOD #3:

**PASSIVE INCOME! You use your money
to make you even more money!**

The 2nd money-making method is quite capable of making you very rich. **But the third method of making money has made more people wealthy than the other two combined!** With this final method, you are putting your money into income-producing assets that automatically make you more money... All you do is sit back and cash the checks you receive for all of your investments!

Now for the best part: our '$100,000 A MONTH SYSTEM!' lets you cash-in with this second and third powerful ways to make money! This makes the next secret possible. Read on...

■ MILLIONAIRE SECRET #71

How Our System Is Built To Let You Make Up To $900 A Day — Or A Whole Lot More — Without Doing Any Work!

Our $100,000 A MONTH SYSTEM is one of the most powerful ways to make money in the entire world because ALL of the money you can make will come from the methods that are responsible for the GIANT fortunes of the world's richest people.

This gives you the ultimate way to cash-in with the same methods that all of the world's richest people use to make their fortunes! The amount of money you can earn has nothing to do with the amount of actual time and work you put in.

And this leads to the biggest benefit of all...

Because we can run all of this for you — it is possible for you to make tens of thousands of dollars a month without doing any work!

Of course, there are no promises nor guarantees that you will make $100,000.00 a month or any specific sum of money for doing absolutely no work — but the potential to get paid many thousands of dollars for letting us run everything for you is definitely here.

Here's why:

■ Your income comes from the sale of the high-dollar, high-profit products and services.

■ The sales material, our proven methods, and our expertly

trained staff do all of the selling for you!

- And you also have the amazing opportunity to get paid from as many as hundreds or even thousands of other people who can also be using the same exact 100% duplicatable system that you are using to make all of your money!

This gives you the power to make up to $900.00 a day or more without doing any work!

■ MILLIONAIRE SECRET #72

MLM SUCKS! Why Most Traditional Multi-Level Or Network Marketing Opportunities Are Nothing But Worthless Scams... And Why Our System Beats All Of Them Hands Down!

Our $100,000 A MONTH SYSTEM is not multi-level marketing.

This has nothing to do with the methods that traditional multi-level or network marketing companies use. If you knew me, you would know that **I have a deep-seated hatred and terrible resentment against most traditional network or multi-level marketing companies.** There are so many problems associated with these companies – I could write a book about it! Oh wait! I did write a book about it! I wrote it in the early 2000's. It's called:

MLM Sucks!

I am in the process of re-writing this classic bestseller right now. It is filled with all kinds of reasons why traditional multi-level marketing is a complete rip-off for most people.

But there are a few things that I do love about MLM...

- I love the idea of "people helping other people."

- I love any wealth-making method that lets the average person make money from the efforts of other people.

As for everything else about MLM or network marketing – I hate it all:

- I hate the complicated marketing plans that are designed to only make money for the companies themselves or the heavy hitters.

- I hate all of the personal selling that must be done.

- I hate all of the lies and deception that runs rampant in most MLM organizations.

Now here is the most exciting thing...

Our $100,000 A MONTH SYSTEM gives you all of the greatest benefits of Direct Response Marketing and Network Marketing – _without_ any of the side effects!

This is designed to let you sit back and make a fortune from the time, work, money, and energy of as many as thousands of other people! You have total leverage power to sit back and make a fortune from so many things other than your time! The more you understand this – the more thrilled you will be!

■ MILLIONAIRE SECRET #73

MILLIONAIRE TRAINING SCHOOL!
Here's The Secret To Making Millions Of Dollars With Our Proven Methods... In The Shortest Period Of Time.

Direct Response Marketing is the world's greatest way to make money! As I told you, this little-known method made my wife, Eileen, and me over ten million dollars in our first four years. We started with only a few hundred dollars back in 1988 and, when the smoke cleared a few years later, we were millionaires.

The same thing can happen to you!

This is a method of marketing that can make you more money,

in a faster period of time, than any other method known to man! It has been responsible for many rags-to-riches success stories like ours. **It has the power to make you a multi-millionaire in just a few short years from today!**

Yes, think about that: **In just a few years from the time you are reading this book — you could make millions of dollars!** Please keep that thought in mind as we continue...

■ MILLIONAIRE SECRET #74

The ONE BILLION DOLLAR A DAY SECRET And <u>How</u> It Can Make You Super Rich!

But wait! Maybe you're asking yourself, *"If this is a method that's making many people like you and your wife instant millionaires, why do you say it is a 'little-known' method?"*

The answer is simple: You see, many people are interested in getting rich in Direct Response Marketing. This is one of the most exciting ways to make money! And many people fall in love with the idea of getting rich with this powerful form of marketing.

But as I told you, this method of marketing is deceptive.

You see, on the surface it sounds simple and, when you have all of the elements working together in the right way, it really is!

However, there are <u>many</u> different details that must be understood and mastered <u>if</u> you want to make millions of dollars in the shortest period of time. Many people don't want to put in the time and work to study and master the more advanced features of Direct Response Marketing. They go into this half-cocked and do not experience the results they want. Then they quit and move on to something else.

I'll go into a few of the complexities of this powerful wealth-building method in a moment. And, if you pay close attention and spend some time understanding these challenges and face them head-on, you really can become a millionaire in no time flat!

But first, let's talk about the good things...

Here are the 5 main reasons why this method of marketing can put millions of dollars in your bank account in a few short years:

1. This proven method is responsible for almost <u>one</u> billion dollars in sales each day!

2. This powerful method of marketing lets you sell to millions of people with <u>no</u> rejection!

3. There is little or even <u>no</u> risk, if you do it right!

4. You can make millions of dollars from the comfort and privacy of your home!

5. When done correctly, a good Direct Response Marketing System is <u>less</u> like a business and <u>more</u> similar to a well-oiled money machine!

The Direct Response Marketing Association says that almost 300 billion dollars are being generated each year through this powerful marketing method. Personally, I believe that they are being way too conservative. I believe the "real" number is over <u>twice</u> that amount.

But what difference does it make if it's one or two billion dollars a day? The point is: <u>This</u> <u>proven</u> <u>wealth-making</u> <u>method</u> is making a fortune for tens of thousands of individuals and companies <u>right</u> <u>now</u>! It's like a giant safe that's filled with millions of dollars... All you gotta do is know the combination on the lock and all of the money inside is yours!

Now listen carefully. Many people want to make millions of dollars in the fastest time and that's great... But these people <u>never</u> stop to realize that all of the money that they want to make is out there right now! This is true for you, too!

Yes, all of the money you want to make is waiting for <u>you</u> right now!

■ It is our responsibilities, not ourselves, that we should take seriously.

Peter Ustinov

■ My parents always told me that people will never know how long it takes you to do something. They will only know how well it is done.

Nancy Hanks

■ Every man values himself more than all other men, but he always values others' opinion of him more than his own.

Marcus Aurelius Antoninus

■ No man is rich enough to buy back his past.

Oscar Wilde

Where is this money?

That's simple: It's in the pockets, purses, bank accounts, and credit card limits of tens of millions of people! All you have to do is use the power of Direct Response Marketing to offer them something that's worth far <u>more</u> than the sum you are asking for and they will gladly give this money to you!

This is great news for you!

Why?

Because our powerful ONE-STEP Marketing System is designed to give hundreds of millions of people something that is far more valuable than the amount of money you're asking for in return!

By the time you have read and studied all of the materials that we have developed for you, you'll know <u>exactly why</u> this simple system has the awesome potential to make you a millionaire in no time flat!

7 Golden Keys To The Riches You Seek... And How We Make It Easy For You To Cash-In With Each One!

The people who make millions of dollars in Direct Response Marketing think of it as a method of and for selling. This <u>is</u> the right way to think of this...

- It's <u>not</u> advertising.

- It's not marketing.

- <u>It is selling</u>!

When you think of Direct Response from this perspective, you will be light years ahead of <u>all</u> of the other people who try this money-making method and fail.

So why is this way of thinking so important?

Simple:

It lets you develop the right strategies and methods that can make you rich.

When you think of Direct Response Marketing as a powerful form of selling, you will automatically develop the right strategies that can make you more money than you have ever dreamed possible!

So what is selling? Here is my definition of selling:

- Selling is serving.

- It is finding out what people want more than anything else and discovering a way to give it to them!

- It is all of the things that you do to attract the type of people who are perfect for what you offer and repel the wrong ones.

- It is everything you do to educate, persuade, and influence people to buy from you and keep buying.

- It is all that you do to prove that what you have to offer is worth far more than the money you're asking for in return.

- It is about building a strong case of all of the reasons why it is in your prospects' best interest to give you their money in exchange for the items that you are offering.

- It's all the things that you do to make people feel good about their decision to give you their hard-earned money.

When the process of selling is done correctly, people will know that they made the right decision because you did a great job of educating them on all of the important benefits of your products or services. They will be convinced they made a great decision to give their money to you. You will have earned their business because you helped them get something that they really wanted.

When done correctly, a good Direct Response Marketing campaign will replace a live salesperson. In fact, the sales materials and systems you develop are better than any salesperson you could ever hire!

There are a lot of great salespeople, but no matter how good they are, all people make mistakes. We have good days and bad days. We have times when we're on top of our game and off days when nothing goes right. We get sick... We have problems... We are easily distracted by an endless number of problems, challenges, and situations. And when you hire salespeople to work for you, there will be days when they do a good job and sell lots of products and services and other days when they can't give them away!

But a good Direct Response Marketing campaign does not have these problems.

When done correctly, a great salesperson will build the Direct Response Marketing campaign from the ground up to do a powerful job of selling. **They will use their experience and knowledge to build a solid case for the product or service being sold.** They will pour their heart and soul into all of the sales materials! All of their energy and passion and excitement for the items being sold will go into these materials and the well-thought-out sequence and methods that will sell the products and services to the largest percentage of prospective buyers.

In other words, when done correctly, Direct Response Marketing is a powerful way to duplicate the highly skilled work of the very best professional salesperson:

- It does a complete job of selling!

- It <u>never</u> gets tired or has an off day!

- It <u>never</u> calls in sick.

- It is <u>never</u> distracted by all of the challenges of life.

THE BOTTOM LINE: Most people fail in Direct Response Marketing because they do <u>not</u> understand that the true purpose of a Direct Response Marketing campaign is to fully replace a live salesperson.

Does this sound too simple?

It's not! In fact, this is one of the main secrets that made us tens of millions of dollars. Best of all, it's the secret that we have built into our ONE-STEP Marketing System!

Our powerful system does a complete job of selling for you. It's like hiring the very best salesperson, who will go to work for you 24 hours a day, to make you the largest sum of money!

■ MILLIONAIRE SECRET #76

The Kindergarten EASY Secret To Getting Super Rich With ZERO RISK!

The <u>BIGGEST</u> problem with Direct Response Marketing is *THE HIGH COST!*

As I have proven to you, this is a very powerful form of selling. In fact, having a hard-hitting 1,000 Direct Mail sales letters in the mail is similar to having 1,000 of the best salespeople in the world who make money for you night and day!

But its strength is also its weakness.

Why do I say this?

That's simple.

You see, to do it right, a good Direct Response Marketing campaign can be very expensive. Many people <u>don't</u> factor in these high costs and end up failing.

But the solution is rather simple:

Just sell high-ticket items that people desperately want, with a huge perceived value and a large margin of profit.

That's it! This is <u>all</u> you do to put yourself in the powerful position to get very rich. It sounds simple because it is.

You see, most people <u>never</u> get rich in Direct Response Marketing because they simply choose the <u>wrong</u> products or services to sell. They set themselves up to fail because the items they offer have these basic problems:

1. There is <u>no</u> "<u>real</u>" demand for the items being sold. In other words, most people <u>don't</u> want them.

2. The items do <u>not</u> sell for enough money to cover the high cost of the Direct Response Marketing campaign.

Our $100,000 A MONTH SYSTEM eliminates <u>BOTH</u> of these major problems. These products are already selling like hot-cakes and the profits are huge!

That leads us to the next major advantage...

You can make millions of dollars from the comfort and privacy of your own home!

Yes, it's amazing – but true! My wife and I started with <u>only</u> $300.00 and turned it into over $10,000,000.00 in our first four years. Who knows, you may do even better!

I can't promise that you will make millions of dollars in a few short years like we did. But I can promise and guarantee that it is possible to get very rich! In fact, there are many Direct-Response Marketing multi-millionaires who make our rags-to-riches success story seem pale by comparison!

In fact,

This is a method of marketing that can <u>easily</u> make you more money than almost <u>all</u> of the richest people in your area!

Consider this:

- You can get rich <u>without</u> leaving your home.

- You can make a fortune <u>without</u> talking to anyone.

- You can get off to a very powerful start for about the same cost that most people spend for a halfway decent used car!

So add it up. You'll see. These main benefits all lead to the <u>final</u> major advantage of a good Direct Response Marketing campaign...

■ MILLIONAIRE SECRET #77

THE MONEY MACHINE MIRACLE!
How Our System Is Designed To Crank Out Tens Of Thousands Of Dollars In Cold Hard Cash And Deliver It <u>Straight</u> To Your Door!

A good Direct Response Marketing campaign is similar to having a money machine that cranks out thousands of dollars a day!

Imagine how it would be to own a money-making machine. All

you'd have to do is press a few buttons and thousands of dollars would come pouring out!

Whatever amount of money you want can be yours by simply turning a few knobs on your money machine:

- Need $10,000.00 a day? Great! Just run your machine for a little longer and it's yours!

- Need $25,000.00 a day? That's okay, too! Just turn on your machine and come back later. The money will be waiting for you!

Does this sound exciting to you?

Would you like to have your own powerful money machine _if_ it really were possible?

Of course you would!

■ The secret of joy in work is contained in one word — excellence. To know how to do something well is to enjoy it.

Pearl Buck

■ I am a great believer in luck, and I find the harder I work the more I have of it.

Stephen Butler Leacock

■ To believe a thing impossible is to make it so.

French proverb

■ Nothing great will ever be achieved without great men, and men are great only if they are determined to be so.

Charles de Gaulle

But all of this sounds like a great fantasy, doesn't it?

Well, in some ways it is, and in other ways it's not!

You see, when you get <u>all</u> of the elements working together in just the right way – a good Direct Response Marketing campaign is similar to owning a money machine that can make giant sums of money for you!

How much money? Well, let me put it this way... I have had <u>many</u> days where my small company in the tiny town of Goessel, Kansas, brought in well over $100,000.00 A Day.

Yes, here we are, a small company in the middle of nowhere (I challenge you to find Goessel, Kansas, on a map!) and there have been many days that we made well over $100,000.00... That's the power of Direct-Response Marketing! THIS IS A GENUINE MONEY MACHINE MIRACLE THAT CAN MAKE YOU RICH! Best of all, our system is designed to crank out tens of thousands of dollars in cold hard cash and deliver it <u>straight</u> to your door!

■ **MILLIONAIRE SECRET #78**

Can <u>You</u> Really Make $100,000.00 A MONTH? The Answer Is <u>SHOCKING!</u> Here Is The <u>Clearest</u> And Most <u>Compelling</u> Reason Why I Firmly Believe That The Answer Is *"<u>YES!</u> <u>YES!</u> <u>YES!</u>"*

Listen closely. I hate people who show off and brag. I'm sure that <u>you</u> feel the same way. The only reason I tell you about the days we used our Direct Response Marketing secrets to bring in over $100,000.00 a day is because... I firmly believe that if we can use these amazing secrets to bring in over one hundred thousand dollars a day, then <u>you</u> can use them to bring in over $100,000.00 a month!

The above statement (and everything else in this book) is only my opinion. But, as you can see, it's based on solid fact! This is especially true when you stop and realize that our new $100,000.00

A MONTH SYSTEM contains <u>all</u> of the greatest tips, tricks, strategies, and basic materials and methods that have brought us over...

$100,000,000.00 in <u>less</u> than 18 years.

Yes, as you know, my wife, Eileen, and I began in September of 1988 with only a few hundred dollars and parlayed it into over $10-MILLION DOLLARS in our first 4 years.

We could have sat back and retired, but we didn't.

Instead, we fell in love with Direct Response Marketing and have been on a mission (Yes, that sounds corny, <u>but</u> it's true!) to help other average people become millionaires with our best secrets.

We have seen and studied thousands of different opportunities since 1988... But our $100,000 A MONTH SYSTEM is our greatest wealth discovery ever! **This lets you tap into the full power of <u>all</u> of the greatest secrets that we have used to generate tens of millions of dollars in Direct Response Marketing.** This is the #1 reason why I firmly believe that YOU can make well over $100,000 a month! Listen, there are <u>no</u> guarantees that you will make tens of millions of dollars or any specific sum of money, but I am living proof that it's more than possible. And many multi-millionaires make our story pale by comparison.

When you add up everything we've talked about – you can see why I firmly believe that this powerful marketing method can make you millions of dollars from the comfort and privacy of your home.

■ **MILLIONAIRE SECRET #79**

<h2 align="center">EASY MONEY! The One Secret
That Can Let You Sit Back And Get Paid
The Easiest Money You've <u>Ever</u> Made!</h2>

Some experts say that *"anything can be sold by mail."* I've heard this 1,000 times. My response is, *"Maybe."* You see, I firmly believe that we are only limited by our imaginations and willingness to do whatever it takes. So I think they are right. But just because you <u>can</u> do something doesn't mean you should do it.

The truth is, some products and services are <u>perfect</u> for Direct Response Marketing and others are not. So why work harder than you have to? Why make it more difficult than it has to be?

Why not use this simple formula instead: Find the types of items that sell like hotcakes for other people via Direct Response Marketing and only say *"Yes!"* to promoting these types of products and services and say *"No!"* to everything else! **It's a simple formula, but most people will <u>never</u> use it.**

Don't make this mistake. You must only fall in love with the most profitable items the people in some lucrative market want the most. Just run every new idea through a screen to see if other people are already getting rich with similar items... If not, avoid the product or service like the plague!

This one simple idea has made us tens of millions of dollars! It can let you sit back and get paid the easiest money you have ever made!

Here's how you can use this idea to get very rich:

- Choose markets that are already making many people very rich.

- Find products and services with tremendous perceived value and super-high profit margins.

- Make sure that you have a complete strategy in place to make a nice profit <u>even</u> if everything goes wrong and your overall response rates are very low.

If you can do these simple things the right way, you can make many millions of dollars, just as we have! And that's good news for you because... **Our $100,000 A MONTH SYSTEM was built around this very simple wealth-making formula!** This is the ultimate discovery that we have <u>ever</u> made for completely eliminating the problems that stop most people from getting rich in Direct Response Marketing!

From $300.00 To Over $10-MILLION! The Secret We Used To Quickly Turn A Few Hundred Dollars Into <u>Over</u> $10,000,000.00 In Our First Four Years... And How We Can Help You Use This Amazing Secret <u>Now</u>!

One of the smartest marketing experts I know says: *"Marketing takes a day to learn and a lifetime to master."* He's right! On the surface, there is nothing as simple as Direct Response Marketing. After all, this can be as easy as running some ads or mailing postcards and sending out a sales letter to all of the people who request more information. What could be simpler than that?

But remember, Direct Response Marketing is misleading... You see, underneath the surface this is a method of marketing that can take many years to master.

This Wealth-Making Method Is Like A Game Of Chess.

To the person who is new to this game, it all looks very simple. After all, there are only six different pieces on a board with some red and black squares. How hard could that be? Right?

Well, as you know, it can be very difficult. In fact you can spend your whole life trying to understand all of the complexities of this wonderful game. Many do. And only a <u>few</u> of the world's greatest chess masters have <u>ever</u> been able to beat a chess software program that runs on a small laptop computer. **You see, within those six individual pieces on those red and black squares, there are millions of different moves that can be made. Direct Response Marketing is just like this... In fact,**

This is the ultimate wealth-making game that you can play and win big!

The people who make millions of dollars with this marketing method every year have usually been at it for a number of years.

My wife and I did make over ten million dollars in our first four years, but we are an exception to the rule. And besides, **our own success was due in large part to the expert help we received** from people like Russ von Hoelscher, Dan Kennedy, and Alan R. Bechtold and our willingness to do whatever these experts told us to do. This is the secret we used to quickly turn a few hundred dollars into over $10,000,000.00 in our first four years... and now we can help you use this amazing secret!

■ **MILLIONAIRE SECRET #81**

The #1 Thing That Separates The People Who Make Millions Of Dollars From The Ones Who Stay Broke. Once You Know This Secret — You Can Sit Back And Make Millions Of Dollars In Relative Ease!

Many people get into Direct Response Marketing because they believe it's a simple and easy way to get rich. This attracts lazy and delusional people like a magnet is attracted to steel.

These lazy people see how simple this powerful form of marketing it is on the surface, jump in with both feet, experience early defeat, and then quit as fast as they started. They go through a few hard times and now they're on to the next opportunity that promises fast and easy overnight riches.

But the people who make millions of dollars are different.

Those of us who have made a fortune know that this form of marketing can be complicated and difficult. But we didn't let these obstacles as challenges stop us. We kept going through all of the difficulties until we mastered the more advanced methods.

These self-made millionaires (of which I am a proud member) are earning the rewards for not giving up. We have paid the price by spending many years to discover solutions to all of the problems that stop the beginner. Now we're sitting back and making millions of dollars in relative ease. That is the #1 thing that separates the people who make millions of dollars from the ones who stay broke. And now that you know this secret – you can sit back and make an easy fortune!

Best of all...

This same powerful wealth-making advantage can now be yours!

■ ...if a man is not faithful to his own individuality, he cannot be loyal to anything.

Claude McKay

■ Honesty is the best policy (but sometimes it has a high premium).

■ Setting an example is not the main means of influencing another, it is the only means.

Albert Einstein

■ When the going gets tough, the tough get going.

But what if you <u>don't</u> have ten years to master these little-known tips, tricks, and strategies? What if you're willing to do whatever it takes, but you want to get rich in the fastest time possible?

What then?

Well, in most cases, you are out of luck. Sure, there are many different Direct Response Marketing opportunities to choose from. But most of them will <u>never</u> make you a fast fortune.

The reason is simple: Most of these programs are designed to make the promoters rich. These people give you a product to sell and some sales material to sell it (usually on a Web-Site) and now they want you to believe that their "turn-key package" can make you rich.

But have they used this sales material themselves? Has it been tested and proven to bring in massive sums of money? Most times the answer is *"No!"* And do these promoters make their largest profits by helping you get rich? Again, the answer is *"No!"* Almost all of their money comes from the sale of their pre-packaged opportunity. After that, they have no real incentive to help you get rich.

But this is one more area where our $100,000 A MONTH SYSTEM beats all of those other programs combined!

Remember, our largest profits come from helping you get rich with all of the materials and methods in our $100,000 A MONTH SYSTEM. In fact, all that you do is one simple step and we take care of everything else for you!

In fact, you can even let our expert staff take care of this one step for you.

I realize that all of this sounds good, but the more you know about this incredible opportunity the more you will see that it is true!

After all, we keep a nice profit for each transaction that we can make for you. This gives us the ultimate reason to do all that we can to help you get rich!

Remember, the more money we can put in your bank account, the more we deposit into our own.

Listen closely. I have always loved to help other people make huge sums of money. In fact, my friends make fun of me and tell me I should have gone into the ministry. Perhaps they're right. But I don't care. The fact is: **I remember all of the pain that my wife and I had to go through to learn how to get rich and anything that I can do to help other people who have similar dreams of getting rich is one of the greatest things I can do!** But I'm only human. And even though I love helping other people get rich, there's one thing I enjoy even more... I love any opportunity that lets me make a fortune by helping other people fill up their bank accounts! This is exactly what this system lets me do!

Our Ultimate Reward To Help You Stay Home And Get Paid Many Thousands Of Dollars A Month!

Many opportunities promise to let me make money by helping others. After all, isn't this what multi-level or network marketing is all about? But as you may know, <u>very</u> few live up to their claims.

BUT OUR $100,000 A MONTH SYSTEM LIVES UP TO ALL OF ITS CLAIMS!

In all of my years of researching tens of thousands of different opportunities, I have <u>never</u> seen such a powerful way to get rich! There is so much for you to keep in mind about this powerful wealth-maker. But the most important thing is the fact that my company can make a nice profit for each fast transaction that we make for you! This is our ultimate reward to help you make GIANT sums of money!

This gives us the most powerful reason to do everything within our power to see to it that you get paid many thousands of dollars every month!

We have taken the best of <u>all</u> of the methods and materials that have made us tens of millions of dollars and boiled them down into a simple system that gives us the potential to make millions of dollars by doing everything that we can to help you make a fortune!

■ MILLIONAIRE SECRET #83

The <u>ONE</u> <u>EASY</u> <u>STEP</u> That Takes A Few Minutes A Day — Then Deposit Large Sums Of Money Into Your Personal Bank Account!

Yes, all of the greatest secrets that we have discovered since 1988 have gone into this powerful $100,000.00 A MONTH SYSTEM!

In all of my years as a professional business opportunity researcher I have <u>never</u> seen a more powerful way that I can <u>personally</u> make a fortune by doing all that I can to help <u>YOU</u> make huge sums of automatic money! Best of all, you simply do <u>ONE EASY STEP</u>! That's it! This simple step only takes a few minutes a day and gives you the power to deposit large sums of money into your personal bank account!

My staff and I have spent thousands of hours boiling down our greatest secrets into a simple system that gives you the power to get rich by doing one simple and easy (but very important) step! We have spent many years mastering <u>all</u> of the complexities of Direct Response Marketing so you don't have to. And it really <u>is</u> in our best interest to do everything that we can to help you deposit huge sums of money into your personal bank account!

■ **MILLIONAIRE SECRET #84**

All You Do Is <u>One</u> Simple And Easy Step To Get The Money Flowing To You!

Our powerful ONE-STEP Marketing System actually contains many steps that are designed to help you make massive sums of money. However, you will only do <u>ONE</u> of these steps. We'll do everything else for you!

I cannot go over <u>all</u> of the details of how our complete marketing system works... There are some aspects of our $100,000 A MONTH SYSTEM that take some time to explain and must remain confidential for now.

However, here are the <u>5</u> <u>FACTS</u> behind our revolutionary $100,000 A MONTH SYSTEM that's designed to make you huge sums of automatic money:

<u>FACT #1</u> — **The company behind our system has developed a brilliant compensation plan that is designed to let me profit greatly, by doing all that I can to help you get started and make the maximum amount of money in the fastest time!**

FACT #2 — **This Company has developed some extremely valuable products that pay you huge sums of money for every sale that we make for you.** *THE BEST PART:* All of the money for each sale that we make for you will go _straight_ to you! You get paid the most money and you get paid first!

FACT #3 — **The Company's brilliant compensation plan also lets you get paid on certain sales that others make for you!** Yes, we can put you in the position to get paid huge sums of money on select sales that we make for the people we place on your team!

FACT #4 — **Our $100,000 A MONTH SYSTEM is an intermediate step between the international company who developed this powerful wealth-making opportunity and our company.** This intermediate step is based on proven materials and methods that have made our company tens of millions of dollars! This is designed to let you and the people that we have placed on your team make huge sums of money without the 3 major problems that all of the other people who are already earning many thousands of dollars a month are making right now!

FACT #5 — **As you will see, there are many different steps that are built into our $100,000 A MONTH SYSTEM. However, all that you do is the first step!** You simply do this first step and we will gladly take care of the other steps! Best of all, this first and only step that you do can be done for you by the same suppliers that we use to build our multi-million dollar company!

So, there you have it! Those are the five powerful facts you must keep in mind as we continue... As you can see, these facts are simple to understand. The only complicated aspect of our entire system is FACT #3 which allows you to get paid up to thousands of dollars a day for the sales that other people make for you! ALL OF THIS WILL BE REVEALED TO YOU OVER A PERIOD OF TIME! However, the thing to remember for now is the amazing fact that all you do is one simple and easy step to get the money flowing to you!

How We Do Our Best To Get Huge Sums Of Money Coming <u>Directly</u> To You!

This is the most brilliant wealth-making system that I have <u>ever</u> seen in all of my years of researching business and money-making opportunities! Once you fully understand how this is designed to help you make a fortune, you will be more excited than you have been for years!

But let's be clear about one important thing: This is <u>not</u> multi-level or network marketing!

I must confess, it took me a couple of months to fully understand how this revolutionary compensation plan is designed to pay you and me a huge fortune for the sales that others make for us. It had to be explained to me over and over again... I was skeptical and my mind was closed shut.

However, my 26-year-old son, Chris, understood it in 20 minutes!

One of the reasons my son immediately understood this powerful compensation plan, and I didn't, was because his mind was <u>OPEN</u> and mine was slammed shut! This is very important. You see...

My son has <u>not</u> been lied to and cheated by all kinds of individuals and companies. Because of this, it only took him minutes to fully understand what took me months to grasp!

But please know this: I was able to get off to a good start <u>without</u> knowing anything and so can you! This is especially true when you see how our ONE-STEP Marketing System is designed to do all of the work for you and then pay you massive sums of money! I'll get to that later... But first, let me give you <u>the main advantages</u> of the brilliant compensation plan that was developed by the international company behind our system.

- To achieve great things, we must live as though we are never going to die.

  Luc de Clopiers de Vauvenargues

- When a man points a finger at someone else, he should remember that four of his fingers are pointing at himself.

  Louis Nizer

- The best way to make your dreams come true is to wake up.

  Paul Valery

- Every morning I take out my bankbook, stare at it, shudder — and turn quickly to my typewriter.

  Sydney J. Harris, on incentive as a journalist

- Only people who do things get criticized.

As I told you, this compensation plan is <u>not</u> multi-level or network marketing. However, it is designed to pay you massive amounts of compounded residual income from the efforts of other people that we place on your team!

That's why I say:

This powerful un-MLM compensation plan gives you <u>ALL</u> of the <u>best</u> things that multi-level or network marketing has to offer <u>without</u> any of the bad things!

The more you know about this, the more excited you will be! As you'll see, with this powerful NON-MLM compensation plan, everything is designed so that we do our best to get huge sums of money coming <u>directly</u> to you! The more money we help you make, the more we put in our pocket... This gives us the greatest incentive to do all that we can to see to it that you make the largest sum of money in the fastest time, with the least amount of effort!

FOUR AMAZING WAYS That Our Proven System Is Designed To Let You Relax And Get Paid Many Thousands Of Dollars In Pure Automatic Income For <u>All</u> Of The Work We Do For You!

Here are the four powerful ways that this system is designed to make you a fortune in pure automatic income:

(1) There is only one basic step for you to do. The other steps are automatically done for you! Plus, as you'll see, the same suppliers that we depend on to build our multi-million dollar business, as well as our staff, can take care of everything for you!

(2) This one step is simple to understand and easy to use. In fact, it's so simple and easy that a 12-year-old child could quickly understand and use it!

(3) You will either do the <u>ONE</u> step by yourself or let our expert team do it for you. Either way, this automatically sets the other steps in motion! (I like to think of this as a set of dominoes that are all lined up. You simply push the first one and all of the others quickly fall down!)

(4) This is designed to make you many thousands of dollars in automatic income! You will <u>never</u> speak with anyone. You will <u>never</u> attend any meetings or pep rallies. (Although we encourage you to get on the telephone with us and listen to <u>all</u> of our special tele-seminars that are designed to help you make the maximum amount of money in the minimum time!) All of the actual work and selling is done for you by our company, our expert suppliers, the international company behind this discovery, and as many as hundreds and perhaps thousands of other people that we place on your team!

If you're like me, it will take you awhile to fully grasp this... However, once you do, you'll see that our system is designed to make it super easy for as many as hundreds or thousands of other people to duplicate the same basic ONE STEP that you are using and make you huge sums of automatic money!

And here are TWO MORE final pieces of the get-rich puzzle that makes all of this complete in every way...

1. Our company will collect 10% of the money on <u>all</u> of the sales that we make for you and the other people who are using our $100,000 A MONTH SYSTEM. We do <u>all</u> of the work for you and earn HUGE sums of up-front cash for helping you get off to the most powerful start. Then, after this initial period, we will <u>continue</u> to do <u>all</u> of the work for you, for only 10% of the money.

Yes, you keep 90% of the money... We keep 10%...

But wait, the last item is even better...

2. All of the money for the sales that we make for you will come to <u>you</u> first! Yes, you will <u>NEVER</u> have to worry if you are getting paid every dollar that's due to be paid to you. We do all of the selling and all of of the money is paid <u>directly</u> to you. Then you simply pay us our 10% commission. As long as you keep giving us 10% of the money, we will continue to keep making as many sales for you as possible!

■ **MILLIONAIRE SECRET #87**

$900.00 A Day Is Waiting For You! Here's <u>Why</u> I Believe That You Can Sit Back And Get Paid <u>More</u> Than $900.00 A Day Without Doing Any Work!

This money-making system is designed to pay you 90% of the money for all of the sales that we make for you on the valuable products that are <u>already</u> selling like hotcakes. Our ONE-STEP Marketing System, our expert staff, and our hand-picked suppliers sell these products for you and you keep 90% of the money!

Since you get paid <u>first,</u> and as often as every week, and since the profits are enormous, then...

I honestly believe that many of our clients <u>will</u> sit back

and get paid _more_ than $900.00 a day!

Of course, this is _only_ my strong belief and opinion. It's not a promise or guarantee that you _will_ make $900.00 a day or _any_ specific amount of money. But I do believe that it's possible for you to make this much or more! After all, I made $10,000.00 in my very first week — before I knew _anything_! I know in my heart that _you_ can ultimately make $10,000.00 a week, too.

I don't blame you for being skeptical about this. Being skeptical is a great thing. I congratulate you for having your doubts and concerns about all of this. But I have worked very hard to try to _prove_ a few of my most important wealth-making principles to you. And even if you decide for some reason not to look further into our $100,000 A MONTH SYSTEM, I'd still like you to benefit from these powerful ideas.

So, with that in mind...

Here is the most important of all of the wealth-making principles that we have talked about and it _is_ the foundation of our entire $100,000 A MONTH SYSTEM:

All you have to do to get rich is find other average people who are already rich. Learn their secrets. Find out everything they are doing right and wrong. Then simply find a way to _eliminate everything_ that they are doing wrong and _expand_ on everything that they are doing right.

Do this in the right way and the question is not, _"Will you get rich?"_ The only question will be, _"How rich will you get and how fast will it take you to earn this fortune?"_ Because you _will_ get rich, if you keep at it and don't give up!

■ MILLIONAIRE SECRET #88

The '$100,000.00 A DAY SECRET!'
How I Made Over $100,000.00 In A Single Day With The Same System That You Will Receive!

Many people are already making huge sums of money with the

basic secrets in this system. But that's not all... As I told you, I also knew that, as unbelievable as it sounds to make $100,000.00 a month, there were many days my wife, Eileen, and I brought in over...

$100,000.00 in a single day!

There are no guarantees or promises that you will make $100,000.00 a month or any specific sum of money. But if our turn-key methods can make us over $100,000.00 in a single day, then I firmly believe that, when you mix them with this amazing new discovery, they can make you as much as $100,000.00 in a month. This is especially true because our system gives you the best-of-the-best of the same methods that have made us many millions of dollars.

Enough said.

As you (hopefully) know by now: Our $100,000 A MONTH SYSTEM is the ultimate partnership between you and our company. You will be doing the one vital step that must be done in every great marketing campaign. This step is vital to both of us. So even though you can let our team of experts do this step for you, it's still very valuable to both of us. More about this in our next secret. *Read on...*

■ **MILLIONAIRE SECRET #89**

THE ONE STEP TO WEALTH!

Getting Rich With Our $100,000 A MONTH SYSTEM Is As Simple As Giving Out A Very Special Toll-Free Phone Number! It's true! If you can give away a toll-free number that we give you, you can have the power to make thousands of dollars a month without doing any work!

Here are the basic secrets behind this very simple, but extremely powerful system:

- You will use our ONE-STEP Marketing System to mail our "High Impact" postcards or use the other methods we give you that are designed to get qualified prospects to call a special toll-free number that we will set up for you.

- This toll-free number is designed to attract the people who are perfect candidates for the products and services that we are making available through this program.

- All that you do is mail the postcards or run the ads (or let our expert suppliers do it for you) or use any other turn-key method that we give you to get people to call your 1-800 number. We take it from there.

- Our staff will take <u>all</u> of the calls for you, and do our very best to close all of the sales for you!

- Each sale that we close for you pays you giant sums of money. Best of all, this money comes *straight* to you!

- You will fill out an easy form that we give you to send the wholesale amount to the international company behind this amazing opportunity. This leaves you with huge amounts of money for each sale that we make for you! Then you send another form to our company – the 10% we charge to make each sale for you. That's it! When the money comes to you, just send in a couple of forms and you're done!

- YOU KEEP 90% OF THE MONEY! We do the selling and you keep huge sums of money for each sale that we make for you!

- Since <u>all</u> of the money for each sale that we make for you comes to you, you will never have to worry about <u>if</u> you are getting paid all of the money that's due to be paid to you!

These are the basic secrets behind our $100,000 A MONTH SYSTEM! And making money is as easy as doing one simple step! Best of all, our expert suppliers can even do this one step for you!

Here's A Whole New Way To Let Up To Thousands Of Other People Make Automatic Money For You!

As you can see, it's simple to understand and easy to use. You simply give out the toll-free number and we do everything else!

Our goal is very simple:

We will do everything possible to sell the extremely valuable products to the largest number of people who call your special toll-free number and request more information. **All of the money for each of these sales comes _straight_ to you.** All that you do is fill out a couple of simple forms which covers the wholesale cost and our 10% commission for making the sale for you. This pays you huge sums of money for each sale that we make for you!

This is the ultimate win/win situation for you and me!

After all, the more I can do to sell the products to all of the people who call your toll-free number, the more money we will make! As long as you continue to pay us our 10% commission, we will continue to do everything possible to make as many sales for you as we can.

It's the ultimate win/win situation for both of us!

But wait, there's more! Much, much more!

■ Most people want to improve themselves, but not many want to work at it.

■ Ambitious people don't make excuses.

■ God will not look you over for medals, degrees, or diplomas, but for scars.

Elbert Hubbard

Remember,

This is not multi-level or network marketing. But it does offer some of the same advantages.

For example, each person we sell the products to may also want to make money by offering them to others. If so, we will help them <u>the</u> <u>same</u> <u>way</u> <u>that</u> <u>we</u> <u>are</u> <u>helping</u> <u>you</u>! They can use the <u>exact</u> same ONE-STEP Marketing System that we have set up for you and we will be happy to do all that we can to make sales for them, just like we are doing for you! However, you will have the ability to get paid many thousands of extra dollars for some of these sales, too!

This is a bit complicated and it takes some time to understand. But once you do understand this, you will be shocked!

As you will see,

This is designed to pay you many thousands of dollars for the sales that other people make for you!

And, unlike multi-level or network marketing, all of this money also comes <u>straight</u> to you first! Yes, you will <u>NEVER</u> be waiting for someone else or some other company to pay you this residual income! I can't wait to show you how this has been designed to make you a huge fortune for the time and work that others do for you! This literally gives you the power to let hundreds or even thousands of other people make money for you!

■ **MILLIONAIRE SECRET #91**

The 3 Ways For You To Get Paid Huge Sums Of Automatic Cash! As You'll See, Each One Is Designed To Pay You Huge Sums Of Cash For The Work That We Do For You!

Here are the 3 ways our $100,000 A Month System is designed to pay you huge sums of automatic money:

<u>**Automatic Money #1**</u> — You get paid IMMEDIATE CASH for

each person who calls your toll-free phone number and then requests a special intermediate package that we provide to them!

Automatic Money #2 – You get paid huge sums of money for every sale that we make for you! 90% of the money goes straight into your pocket – and you get paid first!

Automatic Money #3 – You get paid huge sums of additional residual income that can keep coming to you automatically for all of the sales that are made for you by as many as hundreds or even thousands of other people! As you will see, this daily residual income can keep growing bigger and never stop!

The more you know about all 3 of these powerful automatic money-makers, the more thrilled you will be! Each one is designed to put huge sums of automatic money in your pocket!

■ **MILLIONAIRE SECRET #92**

Here's The One Simple And Easy Thing That You Do To Get Paid Large Sums Of Automatic Money!

As you know, with our '$100,000 A MONTH SYSTEM!', if you can give away a toll-free phone number – you can make money with this entire system! This is the one simple step that is designed to put huge sums of money in your pocket!

Yes, this puts you in the powerful position to make money with the other two Automatic Methods. And, it's as simple and easy as mailing our "High-Impact" postcards or running small dirt-cheap ads – or any number of other easy methods that refer people to the special toll-free 1-800 number that we set up for you! That's it! This is all you do to set this powerful wealth-making system into action!

You give away the toll-free number – we take care of everything else! Best of all, because of the brilliant non-MLM compensation plan behind this amazing discovery, we will put ourselves into the powerful position to receive a generous commission for each person we place on your team! In other words, this is the <u>biggest</u> way that our success is tied <u>directly</u> to your success. More about this in the next secret. *Read on...*

■ MILLIONAIRE SECRET #93

The 7 Powerful Steps That We Do For You That Puts You In The Powerful Position To Make A Fortune!

Remember, the more that we can do to lead each person who calls <u>your</u> 1-800 toll-free phone number through this entire educational and training process, the more money we will make for ourselves! This gives us the ultimate incentive to make huge sums of money by putting <u>you</u> in the position to also get paid huge sums of money!

Just use <u>any</u> of the simple and easy methods that we give you to get people to call <u>your</u> toll-free hotline. From that point forward, we will take care of everything for you these 7 ways:

1. We will send out a <u>huge</u> package of information to each caller – to slowly educate them on this entire wealth-making system.

2. We will prove to them that <u>this</u> really is the ultimate way to make money!

3. We will answer <u>all</u> of their questions and lead them slowly through the entire process.

4. We will <u>never</u> high-pressure any caller or do any kind of hard-selling. <u>No way</u>! Instead, we will let these people understand everything at their own pace.

5. We will do our best to slowly lead each caller down the path to a deeper awareness and understanding of <u>everything</u> that we have covered in this book.

6. Then – when they are fully convinced and comfortable with all that they have learned – we will give them an entry-level position on your "team."

7. You will receive a weekly check from our company for each person who calls your toll-free number and then lets us place them on your "team."

All you do is mail our "High Impact" postcards or run ads in magazines or on the Internet that are designed to get the best people to call your toll-free phone number and listen to a recorded hotline message. That's it! This is all that you have to do to set the money-machine in motion! Best of all, the same experts who we depend on to build our multi-million dollar business can do all of this for you! This is designed to put you in the powerful position to make a giant fortune!

■ MILLIONAIRE SECRET #94

Our Greatest Secrets That Have Brought Us Over $100-MILLION Dollars In Our First 18 Years Are Now Yours!

Our company has sold over 100-million dollars worth of products and services to the huge market of people who are desperately seeking a proven way to make money. We have tested thousands of different strategies and methods over the years and have developed many different advanced methods for educating – training – and selling to very skeptical people. There is no way that I can begin to explain all of these advanced methods that we use. It took us many years to develop them and it would take several months for you to fully understand how they work. However, I once spent an entire summer developing a complete system that let other people use many of our more advanced methods. I spent months working on this project – and I was like a proud new parent when I was finally done.

But my clients hated it!

Why?

Because it was way to complicated! They couldn't understand

or use it. (For example, there were a total of 27 forms to fill out in the back of the huge 3-ring binder that packaged it all together! These 27 forms were all necessary to running the business.)

Anyway, after that disaster, I made a firm decision to never try to teach our more advanced marketing methods. So I began searching for a way that our company could "partner up" with our best clients and do all of the technical and complicated marketing steps for them. This led to the creation of our Internet Advertising and Management Service in 2004 and now, thanks to this discovery of average people who are already making many tens of thousands of dollars a month, it has led to this complete $100,000 A Month System!

Listen. You will discover much more about all of the advanced marketing methods that we do for you in this first Automatic Money Method as we work with you. The longer you are involved with us – the more you will understand all of the advanced techniques we will use on your behalf to educate, sell, and train the largest number of people who call your toll-free number. Over a period of time, many of our best marketing methods will also be yours!

■ **MILLIONAIRE SECRET #95**

How To Sit Back In Your Favorite Chair And Get Paid Huge Sums Of Money For Every Sale That We Make For You!

After an initial qualification period, you will get paid huge sums of money for every sale that we make for you!

This method is designed to make you thousands of dollars a day for all of the work that we do for you! As you'll see, this is the step where we BOTH start making HUGE sums of money! We will work very hard to sell the valuable products to the highest percentage of all of the people who call your toll-free 1-800 number! We do all of the selling for you and you get paid 90% of the money! Nothing could be more powerful! This gives you the power to sit back in your favorite chair and get paid huge sums of money for every sale that we make for you!

But there's more! You see, each sale that we make for you sets you up to make huge sums of daily automatic income with the third and final way to make money!

More on that in a few moments... As for now, let me cover a few important facts about this second automatic way to make money. Here are some things to know right now:

- These valuable products are selling like hotcakes right now!

- These products have a huge perceived value and pay you massive profits!

- These are timely products that people really want!

And last, but not least...

■ Great works are performed not by strength but by perseverance.

Samuel Johnson

■ Ah, but a man's reach should exceed his grasp, or what's a heaven for?

Robert Browning

■ Actions speak louder than words.

■ People often say that this or that person has not yet found himself. But the self is not something that one finds. It is something that one creates.

Thomas Szasz

- We have the ultimate incentive to sell as <u>many</u> of these valuable products as possible for you! As you'll see, this can make <u>BOTH</u> of us HUGE sums of money for <u>all</u> of the sales that we make for you!

I can't wait to show you how all of this is designed to make you and me <u>BOTH</u> a HUGE fortune! You see, the more you know about how I personally benefit by doing all that I can to make as many of these sales for you – the more you will see that I have the <u>strongest</u> reason to do everything within my power to see to it that you get paid tens of thousands of dollars each month!

■ MILLIONAIRE SECRET #96

Here's What We Do To Get
The BIG BUCKS To Come <u>Straight</u> To You!

The fact that people are already getting rich from the sale of the valuable products in this System is super exciting... But even more exciting than this is the fact that you will have a major advantage over <u>all</u> of these other people!

Why?

Because we will be making <u>all</u> of these sales for you! Our Intermediate Step that we provide to you (in Automatic Money-Making Method #1) is designed to bring huge numbers of super-qualified prospects to call your toll-free number. We take it from there and do our best to educate them on why it is in <u>their best interest</u> to invest in these valuable products! We do everything within our power to prove to them that the potential benefits that they can gain from these valuable products are worth far <u>more</u> than the money we are asking for in return. Once they are convinced of this, their money goes <u>straight to you</u>!

You simply turn around and pay us our 10% and you keep 90%. That's huge sums of money in your pocket for every sale that we make for you!

- ■ These products have a HUGE perceived value and can pay you massive profits!

The potential value of these products is <u>very</u> high for all of the people who invest in them. Our job is to prove this to them beyond any doubt and make it easy for them to send their money <u>directly</u> to you! These are high-ticket items that ca make you super rich! The perceived value is super high – but the cost to deliver them (thanks to the modern miracle of technology) is very low. This leaves huge profits left over for you!

- These are in-demand items that people really want! They are part of cutting-edge trends that are BIG now and only getting bigger! The best years are ahead!

The valuable products in this System are <u>already</u> selling like hotcakes! The fact that other average people are <u>already</u> getting paid tens of thousands of dollars a month from the sale of these products is the most important thing! This is your proof that all of this is <u>not</u> some great-sounding idea or a bunch of hype.

■ MILLIONAIRE SECRET #97

The "Modern Miracle Of Technology" That Lets You Get Massive Profits!

With this System, my company has the ultimate incentive to sell as many of these high-profit products to the highest percentage of people who call your 1-800 toll-free phone number! You will be blown away when you realize how and why it's in <u>my greatest interest</u> to do all that I can to see to it that you get paid tens of thousands of dollars a month! This is no guarantee that you will make a fortune every month, but the potential to do it is definitely here! Best of all, we will be using ALL of the greatest tips, tricks, and strategies that we have developed over the years to make the maximum amount of money for you! As you'll see, this lets us use the modern miracle of technology to put massive sums of money in your pocket!

The 10% that we get for each sale that we make for you is only part of the way that we benefit for doing all that we can to help you make a fortune... As you'll see, our biggest profits (and yours, too!) come <u>after</u> we make these high-profit sales for you!

You see, it is the final Automatic Money-Making Method that can potentially be worth a huge fortune to <u>BOTH</u> of us! Best of all, this gives you the power to sit back and get paid GIANT sums of money as often as every week – for doing nothing!

The Final Way To Get Paid GIANT Sums Of Automatic Money Every Week For Doing Absolutely Nothing!

This final way to get paid GIANT sums of automatic money every day is the most exciting of all! As you'll see, this is designed to pay you GIANT PROFITS for the sales that our company does for you and for all of the people we place on your team. As you'll see, this is designed to pay you massive sums of money for doing absolutely nothing!

This method is the most exciting thing about our $100,000 A Month System! However, it's also the most complicated aspect of our entire system.

This final way to get paid will take the longest time for you to fully understand. It is simple in nature and – once you do understand it – you'll kick yourself all over the place for not understanding it the first time... I did. Remember, it took me over two months to understand how this amazing "Compounded Residual Income Compensation Plan" works. It had to be explained to me again and again by several different people. I just couldn't believe it! My mind was closed so tightly that it simply would not believe what it was looking at!

The fact that it took me over two months to understand this was not because I'm a complete idiot (although I did flunk math throughout my formal education!). No! The reason I had such a hard time understanding this was because of two main reasons:

1. I have been lied to, cheated, and misled so many times – by so many hipsters – that it is my habit to be absolutely skeptical of everything I see and hear these days! I always assume that I am being misled somehow – in some way – before I get all of the facts. This forced my mind to be closed shut! I simply refused to believe that it was possible to get paid huge sums of daily residual income from the sales of hundreds or even thousands of other people!

But the second reason it took me over two months to understand this is just as strong.

2. My mind has been <u>poisoned</u> by all of the crazy multi-level and network marketing compensation plans! I have a love/hate relationship with multi-level or network marketing that goes back to 1983 when I was exposed to my first opportunity. There's no room to go into my story here, but all I can say right now is that I fell for MLM hook, line, and sinker! I became so excited during some of my early MLM experiences that I hallucinated! Yes, it's true ! I was so pumped up and excited after some of the MLM pep rallies, and became so manic and animated, that I actually saw things that weren't there. (I swear to God, I was completely sober at the time, except for all of the coffee that I drank!)

Anyway, the reason I have such a deep love for this type of marketing is very simple: **If it weren't for these early MLM experiences — I would not be a multi-millionaire today.**

Multi-level marketing was my gateway to becoming a multi-millionaire. I was a welder in a mobile home factory in Newton, Kansas, when I was invited to my first "Opportunity Meeting." I was 24 years old and <u>hated</u> my job. I hated going to work in the factory and breathing all of the smoke from a room full of other welders. I hated my boss, who was a total jerk! But I couldn't quit because I was making pretty good money. So when I first saw MLM and was shown the compensation plan with all of the circles — I was hooked! I fell passionately in love with this amazing marketing method! I set huge goals of becoming a millionaire. I went to every opportunity meeting — I learned how to draw the circles — and I begged all of my friends and family to join my group. Of course, the first opportunity crumbled. So did the next one and the one after that!

To make a long story short, I became an "MLM Junkie" and joined program after program. I <u>never</u> made a dime on <u>any</u> of these early MLM deals. But that didn't stop me from joining the next one! I was hooked the same way a junkie gets hooked on drugs. My friends and family started hiding from me because I wouldn't stop begging them to join all of my crazy schemes. I was spending <u>all</u> of my extra money on a never-ending assortment of pills and powders that I tied to push on everyone I met. I was insane with the idea that I could become a millionaire. And even though all of my early MLM experiences did <u>not</u> produce any kind of a profit – they <u>did</u> lead me to becoming a millionaire!

You see, there really is a magic to goal setting and thinking big! Those early MLM experiences helped me to catch a new vision for my life! For the first time – I saw that it really was possible for me to <u>be</u>, <u>do</u>, and have <u>more</u> of all of the best that life has to offer. I set huge goals to become a millionaire. I read all of the success books in my library. I also checked out every single motivational cassette tape my library had! I began to fill my mind with powerful positive thoughts. And as my thinking changed, I changed. Within a couple of years from the time I joined my first MLM pyramid scheme – I was self-employed. And even though this business never made me rich – it was a step in the right direction. That led me to meeting my wife and discovering the power of Direct Response Marketing. As you know, this led to millions of dollars. So, even though I never made any money in MLM – this ultimately led to millions of dollars. So I will <u>always</u> be grateful to multi-level marketing.

But I also grew to hate MLM or network marketing (or whatever other names they call it). Many of these opportunities are pure rip-off scams. They promise much, but deliver little or nothing. They are designed and built to make the companies and a few top people a lot of money – but the average guy or gal can <u>never</u> get rich.

However, our '$100,000 A MONTH SYSTEM!' is totally different in every way! This gives you a powerful way to make huge sums of residual income, <u>*without*</u> multi-level marketing!

■ **MILLIONAIRE SECRET #99**

How To Avoid The New Ways That Many Multi-Level Or Network Marketing Scams Try To Trick You And Steal Your Money

When it comes to business and money-making opportunities, there are many lies and deceptions and worthless schemes... The biggest of these lies are all of the newfangled opportunities that "claim" they are not even multi-level! These new schemes pop up daily. They call themselves all kinds of things like "Referral Marketing," "Affinity Marketing," or "Affiliate Marketing." But it's all the same old thing... And it's all designed to make the parent company and a few heavy-hitters at the top a lot of money. The average person is fed a bunch of misleading hype and downright lies to get them into these deals. By the time they discover the truth, it's too late. All of their money is gone and so are their dreams of becoming financially independent.

So when my friend who introduced this opportunity to me told me that "this is not MLM!" I did not believe him for a single minute! I assumed that he had been lied to by others and my mind immediately started working overtime to try to find everything wrong with this opportunity that I could.

That's why it took me over 2 months to fully understand this powerful "Compounded Residual Income Compensation Plan" that is designed to pay both of us huge sums of daily residual income for the sales that are made for us by other people. I kept thinking this was some kind of multi-level scam. Otherwise, I would have understood it from the beginning like my 26-year-old son, Chris, did. Chris was instantly able to see the wealth-making potential of this powerful non-MLM compensation plan because his mind has not been poisoned! He was immediately open and receptive and he embarrassed me greatly because he instantly saw what my skeptical and cynical brain refused to accept!

Of course, thanks to my loyalty to and respect for my friend, I went ahead and made the one-time investment to get into this opportunity – and made $10,000 in my first week anyway. But it still took way too long for my closed mind to grasp hold of this powerful compensation plan.

But I fully understand it now and I can't wait to share it with you! It may take you a while to put your arms around this powerful compensation plan, like it did for me. But once you do understand it – you will be shocked and amazed!